An agroecological food system is no more about organic food than abolition is about unlocking a prison door. In this vital essay, Maywa Montenegro de Wit weaves together ideas from the most important political and ecological literatures of the late 20th and early 21st century. The pandemic provides a focus for these two sources of illumination, but the brilliant light that comes from bringing these disciplines together will shine long after Covid-19's shadow passes. —**Raj Patel**, author of *Stuffed and Starved*

The booklet rings with the question: reform or transformation? It asks, shall we mitigate and adapt or overhaul our imaginaries? We have been given a scaffold for tackling the bastion of colonialism and coloniality and for rebuilding the systems that have rammed a knee into already suffocating food and socio-economic systems. It is time to rise up from a wilfully constructed nightmare. — **Nnimmo Bassey**, author of *To Cook a Continent: Destructive Extraction and the Climate Crisis in Africa* & founder of *Health of Mother Earth Foundation*

COVID-19 and other zoonotic outbreaks such as Ebola are illustrative of the complex interactions between deforestation, biodiversity loss, ecosystem destruction, and human health and safety. These are principally driven by the globalised industrial agriculture and food system, underpinned by the illogic and destruction of racial capitalism. ... Montenegro de Wit makes a compelling case for shifts towards diversified agro-ecological systems that recognise the complex interconnections between human and animal health, plants and our shared environment and futures. Indeed, addressing pandemics systemically, cannot be de-linked from building economies and food systems that are grounded in the needs of people, particularly smallholder farmers, and thriving ecosystems. To achieve this, we must utterly reject and prohibit the ecocidal illogic of commodification, financialisation, and extractivism, as driving forces of human and ecological fortunes and destinies. ... Strengthening social movements at local levels is indispensable towards forcing Africa's hand towards effective and democratic political leadership. A clean break is needed, from ahistorical and technicist development interventions, where technology and productivity are posed as both the problems and the solutions, to an urgent and drastic rethink to deal with the converging systemic crises we face today. — **Mariam Mayet**, Executive Director, *African Centre for Biodiversity*

Abolitionist Agroecology, Food Sovereignty and Pandemic Prevention

Abolitionist Agroecology, Food Sovereignty and Pandemic Prevention

Maywa Montenegro de Wit

Daraja Press &
Monthly Review Essays
2021

Published by
Daraja Press
https://darajapress.com

In association with
Monthly Review Essays

Published in East Africa by
Zand Graphics Ltd https://zandgraphics.com/

ISBN 978-1990263-03-3

Series title:
Thinking Freedom—Series editor Firoze Manji
Moving Beyond Capitalism- Now!—Series editor: Howard Waitzkin

Cover art: Creative Market, Julia Dreams
Cover design: Kate McDonnell

Library and Archives Canada Cataloguing in Publication
Title: Abolitionist agroecology, food sovereignty and pandemic prevention
    / Maywa Montenegro de Wit.
Names: Montenegro de Wit, Maywa, 1979- author.
Description: Series statement: Thinking freedom | An earlier version of
    this work was published in the Journal of peasant studies under the
    title What grows from a pandemic? Toward an abolitionist
    agroecology. | Includes bibliographical references.
Identifiers: Canadiana (print) 20210139846 | Canadiana (ebook)
    20210139943 | ISBN 9781990263033 (softcover) | ISBN 9781990263040
    (PDF)
Subjects: LCSH: Agricultural ecology. | LCSH: COVID-19 Pandemic, 2020-
Classification: LCC S589.7 .M65 2021 | DDC 577.5/5—dc23

Contents

Introduction   1

Box 1. A Few Definitions   3

1. Emergence and super-spreading   5

   The agrarian view   5

   Losing ecological frictions   7

   Metabolic rifts: CAFOs and meatpacking plants   9

   Marx's metabolic rift: a "monstrous expense"   12

2. Fragile food chains   15

   Consolidation, unmasked   17

   Intersectional contagions   19

3. Agroecology for a post-COVID world   23
   Healing rifts, abolishing oppression

   Box 2. Food Sovereignty and Agroecology   25

   Healing the ecological rift by enhancing nature's matrix   27

   Healing social and epistemic rifts with lessons from abolition   31

4. Lessons from abolition   36

Lesson 1 Foundational structures of organizing social life can be   36
changed

 Lesson 2 Reform is not enough   38

Lesson 3 Abolition is not merely a negative strategy   41

Lesson 4 It's important to spar   43

Lesson 5 Struggles always take us back to the land   46

5. Conclusion   49

Bibliography   51

Acknowledgements   70

About the author   71

Introduction

When Cedric Robinson (1983) sharpened the outlines of "racial capitalism" – anticipating contemporary movements such as Black Lives Matter and Occupy Wall Street – he challenged the idea that capitalism was a revolutionary negation of feudalism. Instead, he argued, capitalism had flowered *within* a thoroughly racist feudal order of Western civilization such that neither racism nor capitalism would cleanly break from the old tradition. Rather they would extend it, coevolving to forge a modern world system of racial capitalism dependent on slavery, violence, imperialism, and genocide" (Kelley 2017).

In 2020, COVID-19 would bolster Robinson's thesis, as it moved freely along pathways of international capital and trade, suggesting radical equivalence insofar as no human was biologically immune. It also tore through any real experience of equity, as Black, Brown, and Indigenous communities in the United States began contracting the virus and dying at much higher rates than their white counterparts (CRDT 2020; Oppel et al. 2020). Then, in late May a quarantined world watched a white Minneapolis police officer squeeze the life out of a Black man named George Floyd. African-Americans were reminded that a "return to normal" as economies reopened meant the USA was "working its way back into its familiar groove" of killing unarmed Black people (Taylor 2020a). In what may go down in history books as "Floyd's Rebellion" but was more fundamentally mass rejection of routinized state violence, protests and demonstrations brought communities around the world into the streets in defense of Black lives.

The conjuncture created by COVID-19 and recognition of systemic racism is also an opportunity now to take a closer look at the dominant agri-food system, a central locus of breakdowns in racial capitalism in the USA and globally. Some of its features lead to the genesis of new diseases from agrarian landscapes, including – but not limited to – COVID-19. Other features enable uncontrolled infection and death, as seen in outbreaks among meatpacking plant workers. Still others lead to greater hunger and food insecurity. These vulnerabilities reveal deep and interlinked ecological and social metabolic rifts, which may escape reductionist lenses of most experts in public health – but do not elude a pathogen that, unimpeded by capitalist organization and imperatives, continues to spread. These connections also do not escape a more holistic read on COVID-19, which is my impetus for asking how agroecology can provide critical insights now.

Agroecology is a science, practice, and movement that combines Indigenous and practitioner wisdoms with principles of ecology to generate sustainable and equitable food systems (Altieri 1995; Gliessman 2015). In this article, I use an agroecological lens to look at the COVID-19 story as seen through the food system. In Part 1, I ask: How are agrarian transitions and changing interfaces between "wild" and "domesticated" landscapes helping pathogens spill over into human populations? In what ways does industrial animal agriculture elevate risk for further outbreaks? Part 2 pivots from the outbreak's origins to effects by looking at breakdowns in global food supply chains and the uneven impacts of COVID-19 on food system laborers, many of whom are poor and people of color. In Part 3, I ask how can agroecologists productively intervene at this moment of crises.

Here, I extend some classic ideas in agroecology, where restoring a high-quality agricultural matrix[1] is key to co-producing food security and biodiversity conservation. The matrix refers to Earth's terrestrial surface surrounding its increasingly fragmented patches of natural, unmanaged vegetation – and much of the matrix today is occupied by industrial farms. Practicing agroecology could, I argue, heal ruptured ecological metabolic

---

1. See also: "Biodiversity and Agriculture: Nature's Matrix and the Future of Conservation": https://foodfirst.org/publication/biodiversity-and-agriculture-natures-matrix-and-the-future-of-conservation/; "Should agricultural policies encourage land sparing or wildlife-friendly farming?": https://doi.org/10.1890/070019

rifts in agriculture while buffering pandemic risks (see Box 1). Next, I argue that agroecology must mend social facets of the metabolic rift extending back from colonial slavery through today. To this end, agroecologists can learn from the politics and practices of abolition in the Black Radical Tradition (Davis 2003; Gilmore 2007), which at its core, rejects the idea of stopping at reform, be it to slavery, prisons, or police. Both interventions, I suggest, can complement important methods already proposed to "amplify," "massify," and "scale out" agroecology (Brescia 2017; Mier y Terán Giménez Cacho et al. 2018; Altieri and Nicholls 2020) and help realize radical transformation to a more egalitarian world.

On methods: Following political ecologists who consider the makers of "texts" to be not only social and natural scientists, but also journalists, activists, and civil society organizations (Robbins 2011), I analyze diverse academic and non-academic sources in this article. The research on abolition is informed by organizing work and self-education. I would like to underscore that I am *not* an abolition expert, nor do I pretend to be. What I hope to do is open room for dialogue within agroecology on this topic and its revolutionary potential. Finally, my examples draw primarily from the USA, partly because the scale of disaster in this country put a dark twist on American exceptionalism – in mid-November 2020, the USA had 23 percent of the world's COVID-19 cases (10.8 million) yet only 4 percent of the world's population (JHU 2020) – and partly because the USA is the site of my own lockdown experience.

Box 1. A Few Definitions

Here are simple definitions of key terms that some readers may find helpful.

Abolition : A practical strategy and a political vision: to eliminate slavery, imprisonment, policing, militarism, surveillance, and racial capitalism and to create lasting alternatives to violence.

Agroecology: A science, practice, and movement that combines Indigenous and practitioner wisdoms with principles of ecology to generate sustainable and equitable food systems.

Epistemic: Referring to knowledge systems; in this pamphlet: about ways that knowledge practices can lead to further rupture, versus repair and healing.

Food sovereignty: The right of peoples to healthy and culturally appropriate food produced through ecologically sound and sustainable methods, and their right to define their own food and agriculture systems (from the Declaration of Nyéléni, Sélingué, Mali, February 27, 2007, https://nyeleni.org/spip.php?article290=). *See also Box 2.*

Matrix: Earth's terrestrial surface surrounding its increasingly fragmented patches of forests and other unmanaged vegetation. Much of today's matrix is occupied by industrial agriculture.

Metabolism in nature and society: A two-way interaction by which nature constantly shapes human society and culture (while setting certain limits on possibilities) and human activity (especially systems of production) that profoundly transform nature.

Metabolic rift: A break in the interdependent processes of social and biological metabolism, by which large-scale industry and large-scale agriculture combine to impoverish the soil and the worker.

Racial capitalism: Racism's role in the historical consolidation of capitalism, whose growth and success depended on slavery, violence, imperialism, and genocide.

Silvopastoralism: One of several strategies that reintegrate cropping systems and domestic animal management to enhance food sovereignty and to help prevent pandemics.

1

Emergence and super-spreading

The agrarian view

On 28 January 2020, Chinese authorities reported that 132 individuals had died from a novel coronavirus (Wang, Cheng, and Huang 2020). Just weeks prior, China had identified this virus, later dubbed SARS-CoV-2, as the cause of a pneumonia outbreak centered on Wuhan, China (WHO 2020). The Huanan Wholesale Seafood Market was suspected to be related to the first pneumonia cases reported in late December 2019 (WMHC 2019), and epidemiologists reported that the disease, by then known as COVID-19, had transmitted through contacts with this market (Hui et al. 2020; P. Wu et al. 2020). An open complex of 50,000 square meters, the Huanan market sold seafood, fresh meat, produce, and live wild animals for consumption (P. Wu et al. 2020). Still, the exact etiology of the disease remained unknown. A *Lancet* article in February found that 13 of the initial 41 cases had no known epidemiological link to the marketplace (Huang et al. 2020). These findings bolstered the theory that the Wuhan market might have been a human-to-human super-spreader site, rather than the point of animal-to-human spillover.

Meanwhile, epidemiological need for specificity around animal hosts was not helped by racialized attacks on wet markets. Media reports communicated disgust (Myers 2020) and even called for abolishing markets "where pandemics breed" (Walzer and Kang 2020). Anthropologists Lynteris and Fearnley (2020) explain that in western media, "wet markets" are often portrayed as emblems of Chinese otherness: "Chaotic versions of oriental bazaars, lawless areas where animals that should not be eaten are sold as food, and where what should not be mingled comes together (seafood and poultry, serpents and cattle)." This fuels anxieties of what anthropologists have long identified as "matter out of place": "a symbolic system of pollution through which proscriptions and prescriptions of what foods or foodstuffs may be combined is held up" (Lynteris and Fearnley 2020).

Western COVID-19 media lapsed into this othering, resulting in accounts that seldom included Chinese farmers' perspectives, or paused to interrogate how farmers came to grow "wild" food in the first place. Fearnley, an anthropologist, has followed the emergence of infectious diseases from southern China, often referred to as the epicenter of flu pandemics. During fieldwork in China's Jiangxi Province, he found that farmers near Poyang Lake regularly crisscrossed cultivated-wild divides. They were in fact breeding *wild* geese (Fearnley 2015). Two factors, Fearnley learned, were most important towards bringing farmers into wild geese breeding in the late 1990s: an opportunity to meet consumer demand without illegally poaching from the wild, and a price premium for sought-after foods at a time when rural smallholders faced increasing economic pressure from large-scale industrial farmers.

China's post-Mao market reforms can be sketched as "leaps" (Zhang and Donaldson 2008). In the first leap, which began in 1978, collectivized farmland was distributed to individual households, leading to re-expansion in the number of smallholder farmers, known as "specialized" (*zhuanyehu*) because they focused on particular cash crops or livestock, including chickens, ducks or pigs. In the 1990s, China embarked on a second leap towards meeting the needs of "scientific agriculture and socialized production" (Deng Xiaoping, 28 in Zhang and Donaldson 2008). Heavily capitalized "dragonhead enterprises" (*longtou qiye*) – industrial food production conglomerates – were supported by the state as a means of rapid economic growth (IATP and GRAIN 2018). Schneider (2017, 89) depicts this massive increase in China"s production and consumption since 1978 as driven by an "industrial meat regime," in which modern notions of meat-as-progress articulated with a relentless drive for capital accumulation.

The industrial meat regime also drove independent smallholders out of animal agriculture, especially in pork and poultry. Some farmers discovered a workaround, opting to raise wild animals that could be sold for higher returns in niche markets (Fearnley 2015). Many were pressed into forested regions, home to caves and tree hollows where bats nest. Virologists and epidemiologists studying the "ecology of disease" now fear these trends have heightened the risk of a bat virus jumping to a pangolin or other animal, and from there into humans (Robbins 2012; Wallace 2020). Pandemics appear to track less with China's "primitive" foodways than with its agro-industrial growth.

Losing ecological frictions

Although scientists have zeroed in on horseshoe bats as the likely original reservoir for SARS-CoV-2 (Latinne et al. 2020), the virus probably passed through an intermediate animal host before it spilled over into humans (Fisher and Heymann 2020). A spiny mammal called a pangolin, often sold in China by smallholders, might have been that host (Zhang, Wu, and Zhang 2020). Yet small and large-scale production are not easily separable. In the 1990s, as dragonhead enterprises displaced peasants who cut into forested regions, the social-ecological interface of the landscape was expanded, destabilized, and transformed in still under-appreciated ways.

Evolutionary biologist Rob Wallace has tracked such political ecologies for nearly two decades. In 2015, Wallace and coauthors described how the neoliberalization of West African forests may have generated a new niche for Ebola: "Deforestation and intensive agriculture may strip out traditional agroforestry's stochastic friction, which typically keeps the virus from lining up enough transmission" (Wallace et al. 2015). The basic idea of friction is simple. Neither fully alive nor dead, a virus relies upon a living host in order to reproduce its RNA or DNA. As a rule of thumb, a virus can afford to be more deadly if the probability of its transmission is high, whereas if transmission opportunities are low, the pathogen evolves to prevent knocking out its host before it can spread. Complex ecosystems serve as natural brakes to biological transmission in several ways: through lowering the relative density of organisms, through imposing biophysical barriers, and most importantly through supporting a phalanx of organisms with genetically distinctive backgrounds, some of which will be vulnerable to the disease, but others that will resist.

Such frictions have been overcome many times, disease ecologist Peter Daszak explained in a radio interview (Daszak 2020). His team had traveled to China in the early 2000s in order to study the wildlife origins of SARS.

> What we found was really surprising: a huge diversity, dozens, hundreds of bat-origin coronaviruses. We found evidence that they were continually spilling over into people. We looked at rural populations in southwest China and found 3 percent of them had antibodies to these viruses. And we estimate that the exposure across Southeast Asia is about 1 million to 7 million people a year, just by living in rural areas where bats live. So, it's not just an expectation that we'll have more events. It's a certainty.

That is, viral spillover events are understood by biologists to happen *all the time*, and so the leap by SARS-CoV-2 was, quite literally, just a matter *of* time. Indigenous peoples know full well the non-novelty of pandemics – Old World diseases such as smallpox, typhus, and measles tore through native populations faster than Europeans themselves (Immerwahr 2019). Nonetheless, spillover events have for centuries been geographically limited, snuffing in and out with little notice beyond directly affected communities. Globalization has splintered this general rule, reconfiguring the planet's economic geography for accelerated transmission, including "human networks for potential diffusion [that] are vast and open" (Harvey 2020). As early data from mobile phone users in China showed, SARS-CoV-2 likely hopscotched within weeks from Wuhan to surrounding cities and on to elite centers of commerce: Dubai, São Paolo, London, Paris, Tokyo, Mumbai, Moscow, New York (J. Wu et al. 2020).

Globalized transit is not the only factor increasing the probability that viruses become pandemics. Increasingly, explain Wallace et al. (2020), wild food has become a formal sector, "evermore capitalized by the same sources backing industrial production." Whether harvested or cultivated, wild food is no longer the marginal enterprise the term suggests, and its production now connects megacities like Wuhan to operations at the border of a shrinking wilderness (Schneider 2017). With agribusiness, logging, and mining decimating the last of the forest, wild-food operations must continuously cut further in to raise their delicacies or to harvest remaining tree stands. As a result, argue Wallace et al. (2020),

> the most exotic of pathogens, in this case bat-hosted SARS-2, find their way onto a truck, whether in food animals or the labor tending them, shotgun from one end of a lengthening periurban circuit to the other before hitting the world stage.

Searching for the root cause of COVID-19, then, propels us to look across global geographies, where land grabs and resource grabs decimate the ecological firebreaks that could otherwise limit viral spillover and spread. It suggests we look to the drivers of increasingly formalized wild food sectors, holding state and corporate actors accountable for their role in transforming spillover events into pandemic potential. It also invites us to look beyond sites where pathogens previously held in check by tropical forest ecologies have sprung free to where outbreaks incubate in the heartlands of agribusiness.

Metabolic rifts: CAFOs and meatpacking plants

If zoonotic spillover tends to occur at the frontiers of capitalist development, centers of agribusiness have their own hotbeds of pathogenicity. For example, biosurveillance analysts traced the 2009 swine flu (H1N1) to a Smithfield subsidiary in Mexico (Philpott 2009), a theory borne out by later phylogenetic studies (Nelson et al. 2015). Opened in the wake of NAFTA, the plant consolidated farms in Veracruz and opened Carroll Ranches, where Smithfield avoided environmental regulations to which it had been subject in the USA (Wallace 2009a). When 60 percent of the residents in a nearby village fell ill, the Mexican government confirmed positive tests for the virus, which had by then spread around the world (Tuckman and Booth 2009). Yet rather than belabor the contested role of a particular company in spawning H1N1, Wallace (2009b) encourages attention to the deregulation allowing animal agribusinesses to expand into the Global South, taking advantage of cheap labor, cheap land, and lax oversight. Instead of talking about "swine flu," he suggests, we should be discussing "NAFTA flu."

The H1N1 variant of swine flu is hardly alone. At the Université Libre de Bruxelles in Belgium, scientists have linked intensive poultry production with the emergence of highly pathogenic forms of avian flu (Gilbert, Xiao, and Robinson 2017). In China, just three years before the COVID-19 outbreak began, tens of thousands of pigs in four factory farms in Guangdong – less than 100 km from where SARS emerged in 2003 – died from an outbreak of a new coronavirus strain also traced to bats (Zhou et al. 2018). In late June 2020, peer-reviewed research indicated that another flu with pandemic potential had been found, this time in slaughterhouse samples in 10 Chinese provinces "with high-density pig populations" (Sun et al. 2020, 2).

In fact, to evolve the most virulent and infectious phenotypes, one could almost not invent a better system than the modern Concentrated Animal Feeding Operation (CAFO). Wherever animals are tightly packed together and forced to live in unsanitary conditions – lying beak to beak or snout to snout with almost no fresh air or sunlight – tremendous stress is put on animals" immune systems, according to physician Michael Greger, author of *How to Survive a Pandemic* (2020). The overcrowding and the scale – where tens of thousands of animals are routinely stuffed into football-field-sized sheds – creates what Greger, echoing a 2005 National Academies report (2005, 12), calls a "perfect storm" environment for the emergence and spread of disease.

It also helps to examine the factory farm from the virus"s point of view. The fact that most industrial livestock and fowl have been bred to be genetically uniform serves the virus well; as long as the germ can successfully infect one bird or beast, it can spread without encountering any genetic variants that might otherwise slow the bug down. Evolutionary pressure on virality is also lifted. On a small farm or in the wild, a pathogen is unlikely to regularly come across hosts, so there is an effective downward pressure on virulence. But, as Wallace explained to *Vox*: "if you get into a barn with 15,000 turkeys or 250,000 layer chickens, you can just burn right through. There's no cap on your being a badass" (Samuel 2020).

Underlining that such features do not emerge from "nature" outside and separate from culture, economy, and daily life, Wallace and kindred analysts (see also Moore 2000; Davis 2020; Harvey 2020) take a dialectical and relational view of the metabolic relation of nature to capital. For example, because we are increasingly trading poultry and livestock across international borders, strains of viruses that were previously isolated from each other on opposite sides of the world can now recombine more readily. Viruses have segmented genomes, making this genetic deck-shuffling particularly important. Most recombinations will not result in anything noxious, but when globalization accelerates the rate at which such remixing occurs, it also means an explosion in the diversity of pathogens evolving. In the most palpable of ways, viruses have shown us how nature transforms society, and in turn, how nature is socially produced.

This, of course, is nothing new. Reconfigurations of nature by capital have long given scholars insights into how these pathogenic meat systems were hatched and why. William Cronon's *Nature's Metropolis* chronicles how Chicago became the "porkopolis" of nineteenth century America. By knitting together vast networks of Midwestern feedlots, railroads, and stockyards, industrialists fed the novel disassembly lines of urban meat-packing plants on the livestock of a countryside rapidly reshaped by industrial demand. Powerful "packers" ruthlessly edged out small-scale butchers across the eastern seaboard, who one by one closed their own slaughterhouse operations (Cronon 1991, 243). Local meat merchants found that survival meant selling Chicago beef, for they could no longer afford to purchase, slaughter, and butcher livestock themselves and still earn a profit if forced to sell at the packers' prices. Though meat industry hubs would later migrate away from Chicago, the packers had done two important things. First, they had honed oligopoly power, which still reverberates in supply chains today. Second, they had succeeded in their efforts to "systematize the market in animal flesh – to liberate nature from geography," (1991, 259). To understand the political economy of this separation, it helps to revisit the logics of spatial, social, and material separations at play in capitalist agriculture, or what scholars have dubbed the "metabolic rift."

Marx's metabolic rift: a "monstrous expense"

The term "metabolic rift" originates in work by Marx and Engels, whose concept of a metabolism posited a two-way interaction: nature that constantly shapes human society and culture (while setting certain limits on possibilities) and human activity (especially systems of production) that profoundly transform nature. An "irreparable rift in the interdependent process of social metabolism," Marx (1981, 949) observed, was intrinsic to how large-scale industry and large-scale agriculture combined to impoverish the soil and the worker (Foster 1999; Moore 2000). Capitalist production unleashed dilemmas that Marx – who read voraciously from soil scientists like Justus von Liebig and James Johnston – found not only concerning, but downright absurd. "In London," he wrote, "they can do nothing better with the excrement produced by 4 1/2 million people than pollute the Thames with it, at monstrous expense" (Marx 1981, 195). Marx seemed particularly vexed that much of the nutrient value in this waste originated in poor nations thousands of miles away: the Chincha islands off the coast of Peru. For much of the nineteenth century, both Britain and the USA practiced ecological imperialism, mining guano and nitrates from Peru, and later Chile, expanding the metabolic rift to a global scale (Clark and Foster 2009; Immerwahr 2019).

Urban and agricultural industrialization were jointly responsible for this metabolic separation, Marx concluded in his main discussions of capitalist agriculture (Foster 1999). While industry made it possible for agriculture to grow increasingly mechanized, large-scale, and input-intensive, the developing demographic split between urban and rural society forced a gap between production and consumption. When consumers had lived mostly on the land, waste products had naturally returned to the soil. The rural-urban rift took a renewable solution and created two problems: pollution in the city and soil infertility in the country.

Since Marx's time, two events have paved the way for a second rift to occur (Foster and Magdoff 2000). First was the widespread availability of synthetic nitrogen fertilizers, ushered in by World War I weapons manufacture. With abundant cheap fertilizer, farmers no longer had to plant nitrogen-fixing leguminous crops to maintain soil fertility. These crops, which included clover and alfalfa, had previously gone to feed beef and dairy cows, as well as sheep. With the demand for nitrogen-fixing crops gone, farms could more easily specialize as either crop or livestock operations. Second was concentration in the animal agriculture industry. As production, processing, marketing, distribution, and retail became increasingly centralized and vertically integrated, geographical and sectoral specialization became two defining features (Heffernan 2000; Hendrickson 2015). In the US, beef feedlots now crisscross the southern Great Plains, while states like Arkansas specialize in poultry, and the Midwest and Carolinas focus on hogs. Meat processing, meanwhile, is often confined to a few large facilities operated by food giants such as Tyson, Smithfield, and JBS.

If the first metabolic rift prevented waste from an increasingly urban human population from returning to the land, the second rift has disrupted cycles of nutrient flows between animals (secondary producers) and plants (primary producers) at the base of the food web. This lack of nutrient cycling, in turn, means that ever more synthetic nutrients must be applied to restore fertility to farm soils. Meanwhile, excess nutrients accumulate at large-scale animal operations, with many documented hazards for human and environmental health (Weis 2013; IATP and GRAIN 2018). Dead zones in the Gulf of Mexico, global greenhouse emissions, endocrine disruption linked to hormones in the water supply, the rise of antibiotic-resistant microbes, and incubation of avian and swine influenzas that can leap to humans – many of the ills now associated with industrialized agriculture emanate from this double metabolic rift.

Meanwhile, important debates have emerged about the concept of the metabolic rift itself. Foster (1999) locates its origins in the context of nineteenth century agricultural industrialization, while Moore (2000) argues it is more properly located in the transition to capitalism at the end of the sixteenth century. Moore's timeline more readily coheres with an understanding of *racial* capitalism insofar as it connects the concept of "rifts" with the *separations* inherent in primitive accumulations of finance, land, and labor at the dawn of modern capitalism. By locating rifts not in the wake of industrial agriculture but in the older primitive accumulations that enabled its rise – from financial accumulation in the world market, to landed accumulation in the countryside, to violent separations of nonwhites from their Indigenous homelands – the ruptures are more clearly seen within the long arc of racial capitalism.

I refer to "metabolic rift" in this longer-term sense, encompassing Black slavery, Indigenous genocide, and their dispossessions of land and labor. I use the term in three ways (Wittman 2009; Schneider and McMichael 2010; Bezner Kerr et al. 2019), as:

1. An ecological concept to describe ruptures or imbalances in natural cycles such as soil and seed renewal;

2. A social concept to describe social causes and consequences of different human/non-human relations; and

3. An "epistemic" concept about ways that knowledge practices can lead to further rupture, versus repair and healing.

2

Fragile food chains

Industry has long downplayed troubles associated with the metabolic rift as marginal tradeoffs in the battle to feed the world. But long before coronavirus, it was evident that such agriculture has not gained traction in ending hunger (IAASTD 2009; HLPE 2019; Willett et al. 2019). According to a recent State of Food Security and Nutrition in the World report, an estimated 2 billion people did not have access to safe, nutritious, and sufficient food in 2019. Nearly 690 million people were hungry – up by 10 million people in one year and by nearly 60 million in five years (FAO et al. 2020).

The forecast grew precipitously worse early in the COVID-19 pandemic, with the World Food Programme (2020) warning on 21 April 2020 that the planet was facing a famine "of biblical proportions." More than 30 countries in the developing world, the UN agency cautioned, could experience widespread hunger, and 10 of those countries each already have more than 1 million people on the brink of starvation. In the US, the outlook was no better. Feeding America, the nation's largest network of food banks, said it was experiencing a 98 percent increase in demand – with some banks in rural areas so overwhelmed they had to close. Northwestern's Institute for Policy Research found that relative to predicted rates for March 2020, US food insecurity in April doubled overall and tripled among people with children (Schanzenbach and Pitts 2020). A follow-up study in July found these trends unrelenting: a full 29.3 percent of all US respondents with children continued to report food insecurity, with effects ranging widely according to self-reported race and ethnicity, from 31.8 percent of Black and 30.6 percent of Hispanic/Latino respondents, to 19.3 percent of Asian and 18.6 percent of white respondents (Schanzenbach and Tomeh 2020).

Meanwhile, farms worldwide were drowning in food surplus. In India, some farmers unable to get their produce to market on time fed high-value strawberries and broccoli to their cows (Jadhav 2020). In the USA, Idaho farmers dug huge ditches in which to bury a million pounds of onions, Florida farmers crisscrossed their bean and cabbage fields to plow perfectly ripe vegetables back into the soil, and, according to Dairy Farmers of America, dairy farmers dumped as many as 3.7 million gallons of milk each day in April (Yaffe-Bellany and Corkery 2020). John Peck, executive director of Family Farm Defenders, told me, "Some of the streams here are literally running white now, right into Lake Michigan." Destroying food in the face of famine looks a baffling contradiction. But critics of capitalism as an economic system have analyzed this contradiction many times before. We know hunger is not the result of scarcity but rather of overproduction, with the poor dying because they haven't the purchasing power to register as "demand." (Mandel 1970; Lappé and Collins 1986; Chappell 2018)

Food supply chains, explained DuPuis, Ransom, and Worosz (2020), are generally split into two types: one for commercial use and the other for consumer use. In the latter, grocery stores and convenience markets serve households. In the former, large commercial and institutional purchasers provision places like restaurants, corporate cafeterias, schools, hospitals, and prisons. What occurred amid COVID quarantines was partly, then, a story of food chain silos: as businesses and schools closed and bulk purchase orders collapsed, food that people in the USA now ordinarily consume away from home – the US Department of Agriculture (2018) put the proportion of food consumer expenditures in 2018 at 54 percent – did not have a buyer, nor a ready way to "jump" chains. Collapsing commercial demand meant collapsed prices, meaning it was often cheaper to destroy food than get it to hungry people.

Meat, vegetables, and milk each have particular and peculiar reasons why diverting flows into supply chains is easy to imagine and hard to do. Short time windows for vegetable picking and meat processing, lack of appropriate equipment for commercial processors to package milk into smaller containers for grocery stories, and falling prices for many perishable foods all helped account for global asymmetries in supply and demand at the start of the COVID crisis. But the food system buckled principally due to structural inequalities that have been there all along. Consolidated industry power and labor precarity therefore require a closer look.

Consolidation, unmasked

Corporate control of the agrifood supply chain has received so much criticism that it's difficult to appreciate with fresh eyes the crisis it represents. But the concentration of power is pervasive and growing. At almost every key stage of the food system, sociologist Howard (2016) has shown, four firms alone control 40 percent or more of the market. In meat processing, just four companies process 85 percent of the beef, 71 percent of the pork, and over half of the chicken in the USA (Howard 2017; Nylen and Crampton 2020), and trends are worsening. "There's greater concentration in meatpacking now" than in 1921, Thomas Horton, an antitrust professor at the University of South Dakota, told *Politico*. The first antitrust laws were "passed to take care of the Big Five. Now we have the Big Four. We're going backwards" (Nylen and Crampton 2020).

Reading headlines through these lenses, it was clear that news warnings of imminent supermarket meat shortages (Crampton 2020) had less to do with hamburger hoarders than with highly concentrated industry structures. Indeed, just weeks after the first COVID-19 outbreaks in meatpacking plants were reported, unions announced that facilities responsible for a full 25 percent of all pork production had closed their doors (Lucas 2020). Facilities that remained open – across poultry, beef, and pork sectors – were operating at 60 percent of capacity at that time (Crampton 2020). Desperate to avoid further slowdowns or closures, Tyson, JBS, Cargill, and Smithfield undertook herculean efforts in subsequent weeks to obscure that within their plants, an outbreak of astonishing proportions was taking off. Smithfield reported its first COVID-19 case on March 26 (Mitchell 2020). By August 3, according to data collected by the Food & Environment Reporting Network (2020), some 396 meatpacking plants across the country had confirmed cases of COVID-19. By November 30, that number had jumped by nearly 40 percent to 551 plants. At least 49,454 meatpacking workers had tested positive for the virus and 254 were dead.

Companies responded by invoking national interests. Under the headline "A Delicate Balance: Feeding the Nation and Keeping Our Employees Healthy," a letter from John H. Tyson (2020) appeared as a full-page Sunday ad in the *Washington Post* and *New York Times* on April 26: "In small communities around the country, where we employ over 100,000 hardworking men and women, we"re being forced to shutter our doors," he wrote. "This means one thing – the food supply chain is vulnerable." Smithfield released its own statement explaining, "We believe it is our obligation to help feed the country, now more than ever. Operating is not a question of profits; it is a question of necessity" (Smithfield 2020).

The US government rallied to help Big Meat exploit the pandemic (Mayer 2020). Two days after the publication of Tyson's letter, President Donald Trump issued an executive order that declared meatpacking plants to be "critical infrastructure" under the Defense Production Act – and prohibited their closure by state health authorities (White House 2020). In an accompanying statement, the Occupational Safety and Health Administration (OSHA) all but indemnified companies for exposing workers to coronavirus, assuring employers that the agency would not penalize them for failing to follow Centers for Disease Control guidance as long as they made a "good faith" effort (OSHA 2020). The CDC in turn had no real power to enforce its own recommendations, and as of late June, OSHA had received 5,000 complaints from US workers related to the coronavirus – but had issued only one citation (NYT 2020).

Thus emboldened by the White House and enervated state agencies, the meatpacking companies spent crucial early weeks urging local officials to keep plants open, obscuring testing data, and pressuring workers to return to the line (Pfannenstiel 2020). Thousands of pages of documents obtained by *ProPublica* revealed exchanges like these: In mid-March, a few weeks before a massive outbreak at its South Dakota pork plant, Smithfield's chief executive Kenneth Sullivan sent a letter to Nebraska Governor Pete Ricketts, saying he had "grave concerns" that stay-at-home orders were causing "hysteria" (Grabell, Perlman, and Yeung 2020). "Social distancing," Sullivan added, "is a nicety that makes sense only for people with laptops." Investigations by *USA Today*, the *Washington Post*, the *New York*

Times, and local papers like *Argus News* and the *De Moines Register* revealed a similar pattern of systematic coercion.

In some ways, it all reflected catastrophic failure on the part of the state to safeguard its people. In another way, it showed a remarkably efficient and effective exercise of state power. Roughly 140 years after the meatpackers took Chicago, their efforts during COVID-19 demonstrated that today, to borrow from journalist Schlosser (2020), "we have a government of big corporations, by big corporations, for big corporations."

Intersectional contagions

With consolidated industry power buoyed by an authoritarian state, it was hardly surprising that coronavirus tore through meat processing plants with a vengeance. But for meatpacking workers, alongside workers in farming, grocery, and food delivery service, quitting was hardly an option during the pandemic. Moreover, while in parts of the country, residents ritually cheered first responders, nurses, and doctors to thank them for their service, they were less attuned to the wide range of "essential workers" putting their lives on the line. Many were people of color, connected to food.

Meatpacking, already infamously among the most dangerous jobs in America (Schlosser 2001), provided a ready glimpse into the intertwined vulnerabilities of race and class that COVID-19 only deepened. All types of essential workers faced steep challenges in obtaining basic safety protections, including personal protective equipment (PPE). Yet inside meatpacking plants, the work itself was hard to square with PPE. Joe Enriquez, president of the League of United Latin American Citizens in Iowa told *Bloomberg News* that combining fast line speeds with protective equipment was like jogging while wearing full head gear (Mulvany et al. 2020). Face shields are impractical because inevitably, blood spatters on the shields, forcing employees to wipe them off to see properly and exposing them to the virus. Line speeds should slow to enable social distancing, said worker unions (UFCW 2020). But in April, the USDA allowed 15 poultry plants to exceed federal limits on how many birds workers could process in a minute (Thompson and Berkowitz 2020), and May data showed that hog and cattle slaughterhouse production had rebounded to 80 percent of normal (USDA-ERS 2020). Lines were speeding up.

Workers inside these plants reflect the international complexion of free trade and union-busting that has seen the meat industry uproot from cities with strong union traditions to smaller towns across the Great Plains and Midwest since the 1970s (Haedicke 2020). Today's plants, already sizably supported by African-American labor, recruit heavily from Central America and Mexico (Kandel and Parrado 2005), and recent studies document an uptick in hiring refugees. Nelson and Marston (2020) found that refugee workers in a JBS plant in Greeley, Colorado, hailed primarily from East Africa and from the Burma/Thailand region. Pre-COVID, the situation was thus already bleak. Refugees, undocumented persons, and recent immigrants not only faced language barriers, unfamiliarity with US labor protections, and deportation threats, but had slim odds in legal battles against a $40-billion-annual-revenue giant like Tyson if injured on the job (Schlosser 2020). In July, the CDC confirmed that COVID-19 was bearing down on racial and ethnic minorities in meatpacking plants with a "disproportionate burden of illness and death" (Waltenburg et al. 2020, 888). Some 61 percent of meatpacking workers in the US are Black, Hispanic, or Asian, according to data the CDC obtained from 21 states. Yet people of color accounted for 87 percent of those infected with the coronavirus.

Meatpacking workers were not alone in experiencing the paradox of essential labor under COVID-19. At farm and fork ends of the supply chain, struggles showed parallels and contrasts. US farmworkers were told to keep 6-feet social distance, yet they continued to be transported to the fields in packed buses and have long contended with overcrowded housing, making transmission inevitable (Chang and Holmes 2020). Access to clean water for hand washing was a challenge, since many fields lacked water stations, waiting lines could be long, and workers knew that time spent washing hands was time unpaid (Eskenazi, Moreno, and Voit 2020). Racism has never been distant from these farmworkers' lives. More than a third of California's farmworkers are uninsured, up to 60 percent are undocumented, and federal immigration rules chronically repel immigrants from seeking out medical treatment (Holmes 2013). As if on cue, agriculture in central Washington became ground zero of the state's coronavirus crisis. Yakima County in June had the highest per capita rate of COVID-19 infections on the entire West Coast (JHU 2020), a prevalence that farmworker advocates directly linked to historical racism. "It's almost like we're someone's sacrificial lamb in this pandemic," Rosalinda Guillén, executive director of Community to Community Development, a farmworker-based organization, told reporters (McCarty 2020).

Restaurant workers experienced the flip side of job precarity as they were sidelined in early spring. Until COVID-19 shuttered eating establishments across the country, 15.6 million people worked at about one million restaurants in the USA (Pershan 2020). Of the staggering 20.5 million US jobs lost in April, more than 25 percent came from restaurants and bars, according to the US Department of Labor (USDL 2020). State unemployment websites and phone lines were overwhelmed with claims (Saxena 2020), and undocumented workers – who made up at least 20 percent of cooks and 28 percent of dishwashers (Pew 2009) – were never even eligible. These burdens fell heavily on people of color who now compose roughly 47 percent of the restaurant workforce nationwide, according to ROC United (2019). Women and people of color tend to be concentrated in the lower-paying jobs in the industry (e.g. dishwashing, bussing) compared to fair-skinned workers, who more frequently occupy front-of-house positions (Jayaraman 2013).

The Coronavirus Aid, Relief, and Economic Security Act, a $2.2-trillion stimulus package, was used to beef up unemployment insurance to $600 through the end of July (US Congress 2020). It temporarily helped idled restaurant workers, many of whom discovered ironies of the precariat: unemployment was "a more lucrative and safer scenario" for low-pay flexible workers who lack employer-subsidized health insurance (Stewart 2020). But as states began to reopen their economies in May, laid-off and furloughed workers confronted a new dilemma: they could not collect benefits if they quit their jobs. With COVID-19 still rampant in states like Iowa, Texas, South Carolina, and Alabama, restaurant workers faced the choice of protecting their paychecks or their health (Healy 2020; Proctor 2020). "It's a voluntary quit," Iowa Governor Kim Reynolds explained (Johnson 2020). This "choice" only became more difficult as COVID-19 cases surged across most of the country.

Across the board, then, the food system reflected an economy where race, gender, and poverty had preconditioned COVID-19 vulnerabilities from the start. Black and Latinx people were disproportionately in low-wage front- line industry jobs, alongside women who accounted for more than two-thirds of all frontline workers. When COVID-19 hit, these differences parlayed out into who could stay at home and who could not – atop racialized issues of pre-existing medical conditions, access to quality healthcare, and sufficient income for housing and food. Around 29 percent of white workers were able to work at home, according to the Economic Policy Institute. Less than one in five black workers and roughly one in six Hispanic workers were able to work from home (EPI 2020). As Steven Pitts, from the Center for Labor Research and Education at the University of California, Berkeley, told *CNN*, "To the extent that you want workers to shelter in place, the capacity to shelter in place is racially shaped" (Meyersohn 2020).

Agroecologists around the world have long struggled with such challenges. From ecologies of pandemic emergence to the social inequities sustained by those who work to feed others, they have studied and fought back against the deep metabolic rifts carved by the commodification of land and labor through capitalism. With COVID-19 emerging within and deepening those rifts, the question became, in the words of Altieri and Nicholls (2020, 14), "whether the crisis unfolded by COVID-19 will provide the impetus to change industrial agriculture towards agroecologically-based food systems." In the following section, I propose two strategies.

3

Agroecology for a post-COVID world

Healing rifts, abolishing oppression

Agroecology has developed as a powerful concept, strategy, and move-ment for remaking the world. Much has been written about agroecology's transformative potential (Altieri and Toledo 2011; Méndez et al. 2016; Anderson et al. 2019; de Molina et al. 2020). These writings foreground agroecology as an emancipatory movement to increase farmers' power and control over their own production (Mier y Terán Giménez Cacho et al. 2018), as a pathway to revive Indigenous and traditional knowledge sys-tems (Pimbert 2015; Nicholls and Altieri 2018) and as a science-based way to enhance access to food grown in healthy, environmentally sound ways (Vandermeer 2011; Gliessman 2015; HLPE 2019).

Methodologically, agroecologists of this tradition emphasize participa-tory methods of dialogue, experimentation, and horizontal learning and practice (Martínez-Torres and Rosset 2014; Bezner Kerr et al. 2019). Politi-cally, they advance a non-homogeneous strategy of intersectional alliance-building (USFSA 2018; Anderson et al. 2019), strengthening the grassroots as a space for politics (Roman-Alcalá 2020) and critically engaging and transforming parts of the state (Giraldo and McCune 2019; van den Berg et al. 2020).

Pertinent to pandemics like COVID-19, agroecology offers practices, knowledge traditions, and communities of practice to construct a food system more resilient to complex global change. But the transformative shifts will not spring from crisis spontaneously. I argue that agroecologists have an opportunity now to respond to the conjuncture created by the COVID-19 pandemic and the recognition of systemic racism that has been rendered visible by disproportionate deaths in Black and Brown communities. Previous studies showed that agroecology is an effective strategy for healing ecological, social, and knowledge dimensions of the metabolic rift (Clausen 2007; Wittman 2009; Schneider and McMichael 2010; Bezner Kerr et al. 2019).

I extend these discussions here in two specific ways. The first is to expand our knowledge about the ecological rift to consider biodiversity's role in pandemics. To understand how agrifood systems can be more resilient to outbreaks but less prone to generate them in the first place, I argue, we must begin with biodiversity and enhancing the matrix[1] of agriculture that surrounds the planet's increasingly fragmented forests, chaparrals, and other unmanaged landscapes. The second way is to address racial capitalism as fundamental to healing the metabolic rift.

Some agroecologists have explored these topics. In her studies of the La Via Campesina movement, Wittman (2009) asks if the model of food sovereignty, with its agroecological turn, can repair the metabolic rift. She works through the contradictory relations (class, gender, ethnic) within contemporary agrarian social movements in making a case for agrarian citizenship. Bezner Kerr et al. (2019) expand on Wittman by examining the household social relations embedded in and arising from agroecological methods themselves. Feminist and participatory praxis combined with agroecology, they find, can transform not only farming but also gender and class relations critical to achieving food sovereignty (see Box 2). These studies complement work on food sovereignty that adopts an intersectional lens (e.g. Sachs and Patel-Campillo 2014; Brent, Schiavoni, and Alonso-Fradejas 2015). Nonetheless, race and racism are typically mentioned only in passing, rather than as a crucial component of, healing the metabolic rift and transforming social-ecological relations in food systems.

---

1. See also Perfecto et al (2009) for further elaboration of 'Nature's matrix'

Box 2. Food Sovereignty and Agroecology

While scattered references to "soberanía alimentaria" in Latin America date back to the 1980s (Edelman 2014), La Vía Campesina is largely credited with advancing food sovereignty beginning in the mid-1990s (Patel 2009; Martínez-Torres and Rosset 2010). As the General Agreement on Tariffs and Trade (GATT) and later the World Trade Organization (WTO) made moves to include agriculture in free trade agreements, food sovereignty emerged not as an academic theory, but voiced by those whose "lives and livelihoods are on the frontlines of the battle for control over the land, resources and seeds necessary for food production" (Wittman et al. 2010, 11). Importantly, it was also an explicit rejection of the "food security" framing promoted by the Food and Agriculture Organization (FAO), the Consultative Group for International Agricultural Research (CGIAR), agribusiness, and other members of the global political elite. It comes as little surprise that these actors would champion food security, for "in their efforts to reduce hunger, they fail to question the political and economic structures within which they rose to power" (Fairbairn 2010, 27).In 2007, the International Forum for Food Sovereignty in Mali further outlined the intentions and scope of the food sovereignty claim, defining food sovereignty as:

> the right of peoples to healthy and culturally appropriate food produced through ecologically sound and sustainable methods, and their right to define their own food and agriculture systems. It puts those who produce, distribute and consume food at the heart of food systems and policies rather than the demands of markets and corporations.... Food sovereignty implies new social relations free of oppression and inequality between men and women, peoples, racial groups, social classes and generations (Nyéléni 2007).

Since 2007, food sovereignty has been enshrined in the constitutions and/or national laws of Ecuador, Bolivia, Venezuela, Nepal, Nicaragua, Mali, and Senegal. It has inspired communities from the South Side of Chicago to Occupied Palestine and has been championed by UN special rapporteurs on the right to food, including Olivier De Schutter, Hilal Elver, and

Michael Fakhri. "Rooted in resistance to neoliberal globalization and free trade, movements for food sovereignty are globalizing as well; the idea now inspires collective action among tens of millions of people all over the world" (Shattuck, Schiavoni, and VanGelder 2015).

Communities invoking food sovereignty have created multiple pathways for legitimacy, from making claims on rights and democracy — the cornerstones of Western liberal governance — to expanding social structures, notions of citizenship, and mutual rights and responsibilities to one another and the living earth (Wittman et al. 2010). This spirit was alive in 2015 in Sélingué, Mali, where delegates representing international food sovereignty organizations and movements of small-scale food producers and consumers gathered to discuss their future. The 2015 Nyéléni Declaration[2] for Agroecology, published following the forum, affirms "agroecology as a key element in the construction of Food Sovereignty." Today, multiple grassroots and civil society organizations globally see agroecology as an evidence-based means to achieve the six principles of food sovereignty set out in the 2007 Nyéléni Declaration: focusing on food for people, valuing food providers, localizing food systems, putting food control locally, building knowledge and skills, and working with nature.

Agroecology can do more, however, to make a coherent analysis of structural racism and racial capitalism. Though agroecologists have long dealt with unequal power relations – a recognition inherent in praxis that supports peasant livelihoods, centers Indigenous knowledge, and critiques political-economic structures that shape the dominant agrifood system – overt confrontations with racism are more limited.

Agroecology is cross-pollinated in two key respects when it comes to race and racism. One involves expertise rooted in and deepening among communities outside the academy. The People's Agroecology Process of North America and its members, for example, are advancing an intersectional agroecology to counter "systemic and interpersonal violence of

---

2.   Nyéléni was a woman from Sirakoro in Mali, Africa. During the first International Food Sovereignty Forum, which took place in Sélingué, Mali in February 2007, it was decided to name the network for Food Sovereignty in her honour.

white supremacy and patriarchy" (Snipstal 2015; PAeP 2020a). Second is in the wider sphere of environmental justice, public health, cultural food studies, sociology, human geography, and ethnic studies, among others, where critical questioning of race and food system relations have influenced where, how, and on which grounds agroecologists approach oppression. Yet, as Chappell and Schneider note (2017, 426), despite links made from agroecology to food sovereignty to economic justice, "conversations linking agroecology to race and racism have been less pronounced."

My attempt here is to lift up the solidarity work that exists and press the conversation further. What can agroecologists learn from ongoing struggles for Black lives in terms of active anti-racist practice? How, specifically, does the abolition movement connect to a politics of transformative agroecological change? Can identifying parallels in the prison-industrial complex and the industrial agrifood complex help both abolition and agroecology movements envision how to smash oppressive structures and to affirm life?

The coming discussion begins and ends on the land. COVID-19 blasted through society/nature separations. I therefore first address how simplified landscapes, shorn of their ecological firebreaks, can be restored through biodiversity. Next, I turn to five lessons from abolition to provoke dialogue and mutual learning.

Healing the ecological rift by enhancing nature's matrix

In the late 1960s, ex-farmer turned ecologist Richard Levins (1969) developed the concept of "metapopulation" to describe a "population of populations." Populations in ecology are a group of organisms of the same species that interbreed and live in the same place at the same time. Levins was interested in the dynamics of metapopulations because he understood that in fragmented habitats, local extinctions are frequent – and inevitable – yet are continually counterbalanced by migrations from inhabited landscape patches (Hanski and Simberloff 1997). Inspired by classical epidemiology, Levins developed a new way of thinking about organisms' survival over time based on what fraction, or percentage, of all available habitats contain a subpopulation of the focal species. Just as infectious disease doctors are concerned with percentages of sick individuals, metapopulation analysis is concerned with what proportion of all habitats will be filled.

Levins understood that extinctions were not something humans could meaningfully prevent. At local levels, subpopulations are winking out all the time. What stops the metapopulation as a whole from going extinct is not the absence of extinction of any of its subpopulations but rather the fact that if one forest fragment loses, say, all its rufous-tailed hummingbirds, that fragment will be repopulated from other fragments at some time in the near future. The second insight was that while society is relatively impotent to shift extinction rates, society *can* meaningfully affect migration rates. Here, it's important to understand that migration does not occur in a vacuum – animals, insects, and other organisms move through what biologists call a "matrix." And the quality of this matrix deeply affects the chance of migration, and thus, the chance of overall metapopulation survival.

Perfecto, Vandermeer, and Wright's careful account of Levins' theory in *Nature's Matrix* (2009) illustrates how industrialized farming – pesticide-drenched banana plantations, for example – confront wildlife with an impenetrable matrix for migration. What would it mean to construct a *high-quality* matrix, across which organisms could successfully move, ensuring that biodiversity persists? This is where agroecology comes in – an art and science based on reducing farmers' dependency on commoditized inputs and enhancing beneficial interactions amongst organisms whose functions support, and are supported by, agriculture (Altieri 1995; Gliessman 2015). Because agroecology is principally dependent on biodiversity, it can provide migrating wildlife with forage, nesting sites, chemical-free corridors, and other elements of a matrix through which organisms are likely to travel successfully. This arrangement is more convivial to biodiversity in general, promotes agricultural biodiversity, and is key to reconciling what has been posed historically as an antagonistic relationship between biodiversity and food security objectives (Chappell 2018). It also, tantalizingly, suggests a way to impede viral spillovers.

Outbreaks of SARS-CoV-2, Ebola, and other pathogens suggest that economically driven transformations in land use have altered the matrices through which stochasticity [random effects] in the environment acts as "an inherent brake upon pathogen momentum at the population level" (Wallace et al. 2015). Restoring this braking power, then, means rebuilding agroecosystems, which can look like diversification at field, farm, and landscape scales (Kremen and Miles 2012). Rebuilding may include techniques such as polyculture and intercropping of various crop species to enhance genetic diversity and thus stochasticity at the population level. It may involve integrating livestock or fish with crops (mixed cropping systems), and/or rotation of crops or livestock over time. Around the field, "ecological firebreaks" could include non-crop plantings on field borders, such as live fences and hedgerows. At the landscape scale, while commodity agriculture may indeed rip down forests and destroy many a pathogen by means of host and habitat removal, such production may also liberate many *more* pathogens – "especially those circulating among reservoir hosts that adapt to the new agriculture (such as monkeys, birds and bats)" (Wallace et al. 2015). Thus, at the landscape scale, practices to enhance the agroecological matrix can include natural or semi-natural communities of plants and animals within the cropped landscape/region. Farmers may fallow certain fields, install riparian buffers, and incorporate pastures, meadows, woodlots, ponds, marshes, streams, rivers, and lakes, or combinations thereof into their systems (Kremen and Miles 2012).

Enhancing the matrix through agroecological design also restores nutrient cycling central to the metabolic rift. While Marx correctly perceived soil fertility "as bound up in social relations of the time (quoted in Foster 1999, 375), he understood the metabolic rift to be a spatial phenomenon, the result of displaced people taking their nutrients with them. But a fuller analysis, Schneider and McMichael (2010) argue, would include agriculture in driving ecological mechanisms of the rift. Their emphasis on *practices* within agroecosystems calls attention to agricultural techniques that can degrade, or by contrast, improve soil quality, beyond removing people from land. Among the agroecological practices that contribute to both soil fertility (by relinking nutrient cycles) and pandemic control (by offering an alternative to CAFOs) is returning livestock to land. For example, silvopastoral[3] systems combine trees with rearing live-

3. "Silvopastoralism is one of many agroforestry approaches. In silvopastoral systems, trees are combined with animal production; and in agrosilvopastoral systems, the farmer manages a complex mixture of trees, crops, and animals. All agroforestry systems are good examples of taking advantage of diversity and successional development for production of food and other

stock and growing forage crops – and have been extensively piloted in Nicaragua, Colombia, and Costa Rica (Gobbi 2002; Pagiola et al. 2007) and in Spain, Portugal, and France (Rigueiro-Rodríguez, McAdam, and Mosquera-Losada 2008). Combining fodder plants such as grasses and leguminous herbs with trees and shrubs for animal nutrition, silvopastoral systems give farmers several tools to close nutrient cycles. They can feed livestock with the foliage of specifically planted trees and shrubs. They can cultivate simple fences of small trees to hem in the cattle or complex fences, where large trees grow into full canopy structures, giving animals shade during the dry season. Taken together, these systems can provide meat and milk as food products, fencing material, fodder, and soil nutrients to renew farmers' production, and services such as wildlife corridors and carbon storage that benefit the wider ecosystem (Garbach, Lubell, and DeClerck 2012).

Despite the well-documented benefits of silvopastoralism and other strategies that reintegrate cropping systems and domestic animal management, the scale at which they have been adopted remains small (Dagang and Nair 2003; Garbach, Lubell, and DeClerck 2012). For these approaches and for agroecology in general, researchers now point to "amplifying," "massifying," and "scaling out" strategies that can scale agroecology to include more people in more places while resisting tendencies to strip agroecology of its transformative potential (Brescia 2017; Mier y Terán Giménez Cacho et al. 2018). This work suggests that multiple interconnected drivers are needed to take agroecology to scale, from favorable markets to supportive policy, from learning networks to effective agroecological practices. Yet as described by Mier y Terán Giménez Cacho et al. (2018, 637), some drivers may precondition others: Social organization and social fabric, they suggest, are the "growth media" on which other scaling factors advance.

That is, agroecology cannot scale to provide pandemic-resistant food systems unless deep *social* metabolic rifts are also addressed. In the USA and globally, agroecology cannot escape confronting racism head on if the radical equality it proposes is to be realized. Tensions over racial violence

---

farm products." Gliessman's Agroecology textbook (3rd ed. 2015); Pagiola (2007) defines it as follows: "Silvopastoral systems combine fodder plants such as grasses and leguminous herbs with trees and shrubs for animal nutrition and complementary uses."

have now come to a boil in the USA, offering a powerful lesson in organizing resistance for agroecologists and many others.

Healing social and epistemic rifts with lessons from abolition

The slaying of George Floyd touched off mass demonstrations unlike any seen since the Civil Rights era (Singh and Lakhani 2020). Mr. Floyd, an African-American man, had been murdered on Memorial Day by Minneapolis police officers, one of whom pressed his knee into Floyd's neck for nearly nine minutes while Floyd called out for his mother and gasped, "I can't breathe." Street protests surged over the next several weeks, spreading across hundreds of US cities and towns and igniting parallel protests in more than 60 countries globally, Accra to Seoul, Palestine to Pisa (LFGP 2020). Marchers chanted the names of Breonna Taylor, Ahmaud Arbery, Tony McDade, Nina Pop, and others killed by police just as COVID-19 ripped through their communities. In the USA, protesters occupied bridges and parks, toppled Confederate and colonial statues, and called on public universities and municipalities to divest from police and reinvest in anti-carceral forms of accountability.

Food system workers were simultaneously rebelling. May Day strike actions had seen frontline workers at companies from Amazon to Whole Foods to Walmart striking with demands for better health and safety conditions, alongside hazard pay (Cook 2020). The impetus for this resistance was simple, said Kali Akuno, co-founder of Cooperation Jackson, a grassroots organization in Mississippi focused on building a solidarity economy: "The corporations and the government are willing to sacrifice tens of thousands of us. We have to put people before profits" (Akuno 2020). To Akuno's point, COVID-19 was scything its way unevenly across the country, following ingrained social inequities that have made communities of color most vulnerable to the disease. Though publicly available data on racial outcomes were spotty early on, academics and journalists began to piece together the inequalities. In May, for example, the Navajo Nation surpassed New York and New Jersey to claim the highest infections per capita in the country (Sternlicht 2020). A later nationwide investigation revealed that Latino and African-American residents have been three times as likely to become infected and nearly twice as likely to die as their white neighbors (Oppel et al. 2020). "Of course there are protests," said Princeton professor Keeanga-Yamahtta Taylor (2020a), "The state is failing black people."

Yet while the state was failing people, *people* were responding to COVID-19 with solidarity, generosity, and collective care. Labor strikes and rent strikes evolved within and alongside thousands of community-based efforts to provide mutual aid and disaster relief to vulnerable communities (MADR 2020). Similarly, the Floyd rebellion was both the product of decades of organizing – as UCLA historian Robin D.G. Kelley (2020) pointed out, "We're not here by accident" – and a catalyzing moment for people from well beyond organized movements. Black and non-Black mothers and children, educators and entrepreneurs, elders and especially youth came together to express collective outrage with the status quo. In neighborhoods, churches, city council offices, and the suddenly ubiquitous Zoom space, people were learning about and leaning into police abolition (Illing 2020; M4BL 2020a).

Some changes rapidly materialized. In early June, the University of Minnesota and Minneapolis Public Schools moved to cut ties with city police. Later that month, in a victory 50 years in the making, the Oakland school board approved a resolution to abolish its school police department altogether (Rios 2020). At least 50 other school districts around the country have significantly reduced their use of "school resource officers"– a euphemism for career-sworn police installed in schools – or outright eliminated them, according to the Justice Policy Institute. The multi-racial, widespread nature of uprisings that led to these wins was telling, said Keeanga-Yamahtta Taylor (2020b), and "we're seeing the convergence of a class rebellion with racism and racial terrorism at the center of it." This convergence has revived a discourse of *abolition* that is more relevant to food-systems transformation than it first appears.

Abolition in a nutshell

Abolition as a concept grew out of the slave abolition movement and is now centered around the carceral state and the "prison-industrial complex" (Gilmore 1999, 2007), a term first used by sociologist Mike Davis in relation to California's penal system (M. Davis 1995). In her 2003 book, *Are Prisons Obsolete?*, activist, scholar, and ex-political prisoner Angela Davis encouraged readers to question their understanding – and tacit acceptance – of the US prison system. Davis rejected the idea of stopping at reform, arguing that focusing on making small improvements to the prison-industrial complex undermined the larger goal of decarceration and building societies committed to ending structural racism in all forms. "Prison abolitionists are dismissed as utopians and idealists whose ideas are at best unrealistic and impracticable, and, at worst, mystifying and foolish," Davis wrote.

This is a measure of how difficult it is to envision a social order that does not rely on the threat of sequestering people in dreadful places designed to separate them from their communities and families. The prison is considered so "natural" that it is extremely hard to imagine life without it (A.Y. Davis 2003, 9–10).

Nearly two decades on, society is still struggling to provide an answer to Davis' charge. According to the Prison Policy Initiative, as of March 2020, the American criminal justice system held almost 2.3 million people in 1,833 state prisons, 110 federal prisons, 1,772 juvenile correctional facilities, 3,134 local jails, 218 immigration detention facilities, and 80 Indian Country jails, as well as in military prisons, civil commitment centers, state psychiatric hospitals, and prisons in the US territories (PPI 2020). Outsized police budgets remained consistent across diverse geographies and cities in the US, with up to 20 percent to 45 percent of discretionary funds allocated to the policing system, according to June 2020 data collected by the Center for Popular Democracy (CPD 2020).

Movements to abolish this swelling carceral apparatus came to prominence in California in the 1990s with the founding of the Critical Resistance project, a national anti-prison organization with an abolitionist focus co-founded by Angela Davis and professor Ruth Wilson Gilmore. Today, Critical Resistance (CR) operates from an explicitly intersectional racial-justice lens, in which abolition counters the many ways power is collected and maintained through the prison-industrial complex, "including creating mass media images that keep alive stereotypes of people of color, poor people, queer people, immigrants, youth, and other oppressed communities as criminal, delinquent, or deviant" (CR 2020). This power, explains CR (2020), is consolidated through several channels: earning exorbitant profits for private companies, securing political gains for "tough on crime" politicians, enhancing the influence of police and prison guard unions, and "eliminating social and political dissent by oppressed communities that make demands for self-determination and reorganization of power in the US" (A.Y. Davis 2003).

For scholars of the Black Radical Tradition, the work undertaken by Critical Resistance, Dignity and Power, and other grassroots organizations grows from an understanding of "racial capitalism," a concept Robinson (1983) expanded to a generalized analysis of racism's role in the historical consolidation of capitalism. For Robinson, capitalism and racism did not break from the old feudal order but rather evolved from it to produce a modern world system of racial capitalism dependent on slavery, violence, imperialism, and genocide. Abolition, then, in the words of Johnson and Lubin (2017, 12):

> entails not only the end of racial slavery, racial segregation, and racism, but the abolition of a capitalist order that has always been racial, and that not only extracts life from Black bodies but dehumanizes all workers while colonizing indigenous lands and incarcerating surplus bodies.

It was W.E.B. Du Bois, Johnson and Lubin suggest, who was the first to discuss (though not enact) abolitionism in this larger sense. Du Bois saw abolition democracy during the era of Reconstruction as a political struggle for collective liberation, bringing freedom to both Black and white workers in the form of redistributed wealth, free public education across the working poor, and for many, the right to vote.

In short, abolition is a practical strategy and a political vision: to eliminate imprisonment, policing, militarism, and surveillance and to create lasting alternatives to violence. As a set of political beliefs, it isn't only about "throwing the prison doors wide open," as CR explains, but creating "new models for living" (CR 2012, 27); abolitionists seek to build a world *with* in order to achieve a world without. In practical terms, strategies include divesting from police and prisons in order to reinvest in community self-governance and care, mental health aids, trauma counselors, and neighborhood violence interrupters (8toAbolition 2020). It involves repealing laws that criminalize survival to stanch the flow of people need-lessly pulled into the criminal punishment system. Summoning Du Bois, abolitionists demand collective liberation through securing what racial capitalism does not: access to safe and affordable housing, high-quality healthcare, and nourishing, culturally appropriate food; access to non-proprietary modes of sharing information; and access to an intellectual commons in which workers, students, community members, and acade-mics are all equally valued and centered in a vision of educational futures (COC 2020). These are all elements of what abolitionists consider pre-con-ditions for a violence-free life.

4

Lessons from abolition

Abolition is, I argue, an important concept for agroecologists to consider, learn from, and live into. Though books can be written on the topic, I offer here a few brief examples of crossover struggles with lessons agroecologists can glean.

Lesson 1
Foundational structures of organizing social life can be changed

> Slavery, lynching, and segregation are certainly compelling examples of social institutions that, like the prison, were once considered to be as everlasting as the sun (Davis 2003, 24).

First, abolition is fundamentally about rejecting the idea that foundational structures of organizing social life are solid, natural, or unchangeable. Abolitionists remind us that institutions such as slavery, lynching, and Jim Crow laws were once considered normal and "natural."

> When Frederick Douglass embarked on his career as an antislavery orator, white people – even those who were passionate abolitionists – refused to believe that a black slave could display such intelli-

gence. The belief in the permanence of slavery was so widespread that even white abolitionists found it difficult to imagine black people as equals (Davis 2003, 23).

It took a bloody Civil War to legally dissolve the "peculiar institution" of slavery. Even then, as depicted in DuVernay's (2016) film, the 13th Amendment contained a devastating caveat: "Neither slavery nor involuntary servitude, *except as a punishment for crime whereof the party shall have been duly convicted*, shall exist within the United States."

This loophole provided pretext for police to arrest poor freedmen and force them to work for the state under convict leasing, a system in which companies and plantation owners leased prisoners to build railroads and to perform agricultural labor (Haley 2016, 17–118). Convict leasing, lynching, and disenfranchisement, in turn, were toppled with relentless efforts of movements led by figures such as Ida B. Wells, Selena Sloan Butler, Mary Church Terrell, and activists in the Student Nonviolent Coordinating Committee – including a young sharecropper named Fannie Lou Hamer (White 2018, 65–87). In a speech delivered to the 1964 Democratic National Convention, Hamer shared her own experience with state-sanctioned violence, including a police beating that permanently damaged her eyesight and kidneys (Hamer 1964).

> Is this America, the land of the free and the home of the brave, where we have to sleep with our telephones off the hooks because our lives be threatened daily, because we want to live as decent human beings, in America? she asked.

The Voting Rights Act of 1965 was signed into law by President Lyndon B. Johnson the following year.

The double edge of this pen stroke and others like it was the swiftness with which governments, corporations, and mainstream media have moved to represent racism as a thing of the past. Black women CEOs and Black men in the Oval Office are held up as symbols of a postracial society, obscuring the structural racism that today stretches from the ecology of urban landscapes (Schell et al. 2020) to patterns of COVID-19 infection and mortality. At the same time, as Angela Davis wrote nearly 20 years ago, "anyone who would dare to call for the reintroduction of slavery, the organization of lynch mobs, or the reestablishment of legal segregation would be summarily dismissed" (Davis 2003, 24). Racist institutions, in other words, were far more vulnerable than anyone would have imagined. We have seen *dramatic* change in the past because people insisted on abolition.

Translated into food system terms, agroecologists should be heartened that the everlasting suns of the long Green Revolution and corporate food regime are indeed vulnerable. Liberalized trade, free markets, financialization, and private property rights in land, water, animals, and seeds can be destabilized. The systematic cheapening of nature, labor, care, and lives that renders food so cheap can be delegitimized just as slavery (the original cheap lives institution) was. What appears radical now, in terms of practicing biodiversity-based farming, establishing worker-owned farming and food cooperatives, and enacting agency and power in agrifood governance can evolve into commonsense.

How? Abolition history shows that this evolution, while possible, is not "natural"; new normals were not reestablished without sustained counter-hegemonic organizing – and people willing to take risks. Hamer, for example, is often recalled for her electoral activism. But the greater risk she and others took was to demand that the state support changes that communities were already making. In founding the Mississippi Freedom Farms Cooperative, she saw the community as a site of effective governance, where Black farmers could enact a prefigurative politics of collective ownership, collective care, and self-determination. Such retractions from using and participating in dominant systems undermine the core dependencies on which any oppressive system feeds, therein shifting the grounds for emancipatory strategies like abolition and agroecology to take hold.

Lesson 2
Reform is not enough

It follows, then, that agroecologists must resist the impulse to simply reform oppressive structures. No, says abolition. Reform is not borne up by the evidence. "There is not a single era in United States history in which the police were not a force of violence against black people," wrote

Kaba (2020), a longtime abolition organizer and educator, in the *New York Times*. From slave patrols of the 1700 and 1800s through strike-break-ing police departments of the mid-19th century, police have always sup-pressed marginalized people to protect the status quo. Yet, surely enough, in the aftermath of Mr. Floyd's killing, many reformist responses surfaced. Universities scrambled to assemble new task forces populated by minority stakeholders. Police departments pledged to revisit chokeholds as a form of restraint. A campaign called #8Can'tWait gathered inertia on social media, garnering celebrity endorsements; its pillars included banning chokeholds, requiring warning before shooting, and other remedies billed as effective, no-cost, and easy to implement (Yglesias 2020).

Some events revealed the attractive skin in which reformism often comes. At the University of California-Los Angeles, faculty organized a Divest/Invest Collective and called on their university to end the univer-sity's relationship with the LA Police Department, defund the UC Police Department, and redirect resources toward racial and gender justice teach- ing and anti-carceral forms of accountability. "We want to be clear," they wrote (UCLA 2020):

> this is not a call for police reform or better training or kinder and gentler approaches such as community policing. A national, indeed global, commonsense is taking shape, rejecting such reform.

The university was quick to respond with a proposal for reform wrapped in the corporate language of diversity. As Black Studies professor Robin D.G. Kelley explained, UCLA promised to review the campus relationship with other police forces, discuss joint training for UCPD and LAPD, and undertake implicit bias and deescalation training. In other words, he said, "all these things that don't work" (SSJ 2020). In addition, Kelley cautioned about the administration's tactical moves "to split our ranks." They do this all the time, he said. "They offer resources for Black Studies and Ethnic Studies in exchange for discarding the demands to abolish the police." Choices are presented as a zero-sum game in which faculty lines, better pay, and fancier offices are offered as the realistic alternatives to the thing (abolition) that isn't realistic. Kelley asked (SSJ 2020): "Who's going to go for the bribe? And are we going to hold on for real structural change?"

Agroecologists can learn from these experiences in their own struggles between reform and transformation (Holt Giménez and Shattuck 2011). Within the past decade, agroecology has gained new popularity, with everyone from CropLife, a trade group representing the agrochemical industry, to the UN Food and Agriculture Organization newly embracing its terms, if not always its tenets. As Giraldo and Rosset (2018, 546) observe: "Agroecology has gone from being ignored, ridiculed and/or excluded by the large institutions that preside over world agriculture to being recognized as one of the possible alternatives available to address the crises caused by the Green Revolution." These developments present risks but also openings for agroecologists and their allies. What is reform? What is transformation? What incremental changes, not to be confused with merely adjusting the status quo, can work slowly to overturn, unlock, and open up space for enduring alternatives to grow? Kelley's words should ring in the ears of agroecologists. *"Who's going to go for the bribe? And are we going to hold on for real structural change?"*

With this provocation, it's possible to survey the landscape of food movement struggles with a more critical eye. Movement wins have resulted in better pay for some fast-food workers and farmworkers ($15 an hour and a penny-per-pound, respectively), in more organic options at the supermarket, in paid sick leave and protective gear for meatpacking workers, in economic incentives to protect soil health, and in agriculture's inclusion in the Green New Deal. Yet these wins easily become piecemeal reforms if perceived as endpoints, rather than as steps on a convoluted path toward structural transformation. Without such an analysis, it becomes all too easy to mistake winning with a little less abuse. We begin to count victory as masks for people chained to disassembly lines of factory-farmed animals, rather than asking if that system makes any sense. We forget how efficiently large-scale landowners gain an advantage in any commodified system, including carbon payments. We treat the USA as an island that can "go green" in isolation, without facing the political-economic reality in which primitive accumulation always opens new frontiers, and environmental resources – like Bolivian lithium, prized for making batteries – never come from nowhere.

What does this mean for agroecology gaining more institutional recognition? A concern expressed by Giraldo and Rosset (2018, 545) is the strong risk that "agroecology will be co-opted, institutionalized, colonized and stripped of its political content." They also recognize, however, that if agroecology is a territory in dispute, social movements can avail themselves of agroecology's rising popularity to make substantive changes in the food system. Lessons from abolition suggest that agroecology movements will need not only to apply concerted pressure but also to advance clear political proposals. Where abolition demands defunding the police, eliminating prisons, and dissolving the associated legal apparatus of criminal justice, agroecology proposals will need to specify analogous, non-negotiable termination of the many discrete, yet "locked in" elements of the industrial agrifood regime. Borrowing from an analysis by IPES-Food (2016), these include: an end to the export orientation of agricultural markets imposed on many countries, particularly in the global South; an end to measures of success cast in a productionist mold that cannot see success in other terms; an end to compartmentalised and reductionist thinking that cannot accommodate relational, ecological understandings and world views; and an end to the Malthusian mantra of "feeding the world" which, like a zombie, has long been dead but haunts us still. Beyond what IPES proposed, it includes appreciating that the concentration of power in food systems is and has always been racialized. If so, then an abolitionist agroecology must demand, as a non-negotiable, that all forms of oppression must go.

Lesson 3
Abolition is not merely a negative strategy

> Abolition is about presence, not absence. It's about building life-affirming institutions. (Gilmore, in MPD150 2020)

In the tradition of abolitionists like Angela Davis and Ruth Gilmore, abolition is never simply about dismantling, or getting rid of, systems of violence. It is about reimagining and building the world anew. These visions, moreover, are brought down to earth with practical strategies to reallocate resources that already exist. "We call on localities and elected officials across the country to divest resources away from policing in local budgets and reallocate those resources to the healthcare, housing and education our people deserve," says the Movement for Black Lives in its Divest/Invest action toolkit (M4BL 2020b). Shifting funds from a police department like New York City's can free up tremendous resources for community-led solutions. According to the Center for Popular Democracy (2020), the New York Police Department budget is nearly $6 billion and the Los Angeles Police Department has a 2020 budget of $1.7 billion, accounting for more than a quarter of the city's general fund. Resources are not scarce, in other words. They're only, as Gilmore argues (2007), sequestered within and by a prison-industrial complex that functions to maintain an unjust social order by securing and mobilizing surplus finance capital, land, labor, and state capacity. Abolitionists ask: what if instead, we *redirect* these substantial resources toward building life-affirming solutions?

Agroecologists know the legacy of underinvestment all too well. Path-dependent processes in agricultural research that inscribe technological regimes now readily develop some solutions (like genetic engineering) but lock out others, including agroecology (Vanloqueren and Baret 2009). According to research by DeLonge, Miles, and Carlisle (2016), the total US Department of Agriculture budget in 2014 was about $157.5 billion. Of this total, the agency spent roughly $294 million on grants for research, extension, and education in agriculture. Of that sum, a mere $12 million went to projects with transformative agroecology potential, meaning integrating social with ecological aspects. In university systems, agroecology has been part of a systematic defunding of research antithetical to the objectives of industrial agriculture. Biocontrol research in the University of California system, for example, once had its own departments, research facilities, and faculty at UC Berkeley, UC Riverside, and UC Davis, combined with an experiment station at the Albany Gill Tract (Warner et al. 2011). From the 1920s through the 1970s, this infrastructure generated scientific evidence of effective pest control; produced numerous graduate students who became research leaders at other universities and government agencies; and generated demonstrable economic benefits for California agriculture. But hand-in-glove with the 1970s neoliberal turn, biological control, along with other applied biology departments, was slowly dismantled in favor of investments in molecular biology and genetics (Buttel 2005).

A divest/invest strategy for agroecology is therefore both ideological, about the explicit and intentional articulation of defensive and offensive approaches, and practical, about redirecting money and other resources from where they have been accumulated so effectively by agribusiness. It is about demanding from our public institutions that resources be channeled towards agroecological alternatives so that it becomes realistic to go from niche to paradigm-shifting potential (IPES-Food 2016). It is about chronicling the evidence: significant improvements to maternal and child nutrition, food security, crop diversity, and gender equality in places like Malawi and Cuba thanks to agroecology in the context of participatory education (Bezner Kerr, Berti, and Shumba 2011; Rosset et al. 2011); enhancements to climate and economic disaster resilience in places like Puerto Rico and Guatemala among smallholders practicing agroecology (Calderón et al. 2018; Álvarez Febles and Félix 2020); and benefits to rural incomes and employment in parts of Latin America and Europe where agroecological production mutually transforms economic organization (Mier y Terán Giménez Cacho et al. 2018; van der Ploeg et al. 2019). It is also honesty about agroecology's remaining unknowns and deficiencies – e.g., undone science, limited public infrastructure, scant supportive policy, and threats from agribusiness interests – which will not weaken the argument for divestment and investment but rather should strengthen it.

Lesson 4
It's important to spar

> solidarity is something that is made and remade and remade. It never just is (Gilmore 2020).

Most abolitionists and agroecologists have heard some version of the response: "Isn't that unrealistic?" Skeptics in the USA who worry that safe schools and universities are impossible without police are often surprised to learn that nearly all countries on Earth have already achieved this feat. People who ask if agroecology can feed the world either have not heard about or ignore the fact that small-scale diversified agriculture fed most pre-industrial societies, including advanced civilizations. They may not know agroecology is feeding people today, even as dominant food systems fail them.

To take a recent example, Puerto Rico was already deeply vulnerable before Hurricane María struck in 2017. The island imports nearly 85 percent of its food, the result of its local farming being displaced by US-led sugar plantations and industrialization (Gies 2018). When the hurricane killed more than 3,000 people and the US government failed to respond, local residents mobilized to help one another rebuild. Among these was the Organización Boricuá de Agricultura Ecológica, which alongside other Puerto Rican organizations, cleared roads, rebuilt farms, and delivered food (root crops survived the hurricane's 140 mph winds) to desperate rural communities through a coordinated system of Food Sovereignty Brigades that carried people and supplies on the 'Guagua Solidaria' (Solidarity Bus). During COVID-19, many similar examples of agroecological resilience surfaced: from Indigenous communities of the Great Lakes Basin revitalizing native seed networks (Uyeda 2020) to the Landless Workers Movement of Brazil channeling their agroecological capacity to give over 500 tons of produce to hospitals and poor neighborhoods, transform urban cafes into soup kitchens for the homeless, and convert some education buildings into makeshift hospitals staffed in part by its 130 affiliated doctors (Tarlau 2020). When agroecologists, like abolitionists, hear that their plans are simply not realistic, the answer can and should be: in spite of everything, it is *already* real.

Also real is the struggle through which this ability to be resilient is born. Struggle not only manifests against one's oppressors, be they right-wing authoritarians in Brazil, US austerity politics in Puerto Rico, or prisons into which debtors, Indigenous peoples, and others deemed deviant are easily thrown. The struggle to survive, amplify, and win also happens on the inside: within and between overlapping constituencies with shared commitments but varied understandings of what winning looks like, and which specific strategies and tactics will work to achieve it. Here again, agroecology has much to learn from and share with abolition.

"It's important to spar, and to work out our differences," said Gilmore at the 2019 MUMI abolition conference in Mississippi, making the point that not everyone in the room – and certainly not everyone in the abolitionist movement – is on the same page, and that there's no need to pretend otherwise (Herskind 2019). Gilmore was not encouraging a watering-down of abolition – to the contrary, she and others actively reject such dilution. She was, however, encouraging an approach that is critical and relevant to agroecology, as it expands into new geographical, institutional, and cultural spaces. People need to spar, to disagree, to work out their differences as they build – and in order to build – together. The action and *interaction*, moreover, uplifts abolish as a verb. Neither "agroecologists" nor "abolitionists" should be as much about identity as about *doing*. Neither represent plans to be sketched out on paper and then implemented wholesale. Both must be practiced and lived, worked and reworked.

In this reworking, abolition and agroecology stop being realms to cross-compare and start being movements and ideologies that can grow into one another. Epistemically, a shared analysis of class and race embodied in "racial capitalism" anoints their causes and commitments as one – in order to be anti-racist, the struggle involves a transformation of the political economic order. In order to transform foundations of economic life, the struggle requires eradicating racism. Strategically, it suggests strengthening the coalitional networks that link abolition and agroecology. Movements against policing and the carceral state could be wedded to movements for economic justice and self-determination, including, at their base, the ability to feed ourselves from the land. Ending systemic racism, they would show, involves healing the ecological rift, not just the social and epistemic. Political education could connect prisons and farms to classrooms and kitchens, seizing on the power of education to shape collective action: What is the history of this condition? What do we know – and not know? How can we build a world, broken loose from carceral logics, that nurtures and grows from an ethic of care?

The People's Agroecology Process (PAeP) is one arena where such visions are percolating. Born of a strategy to "bypass the influence of the non-profit industrial complex" in North America, PAeP has grown since 2014 via place-based "encounters" designed to build a shared analysis with international movements, forge stronger grassroots relationships, and promote mutual learning (PAeP 2020a, 5, 13). People who have participated in the encounters attest that they're far from ordinary conference events. "We live together, feed one another, work the land together. We live in community, recognize the time and the history of the territory in which we are meeting," said Jesús Vázquez of Organización Boricuá (PAeP 2020b). PAeP's larger goal, as expressed by Kathia Ramírez of the Farmworker Support Committee (PAeP 2020a, 5), is to "amplify the struggles taking place within different communities" and to generate "conversations that we don't often have, because we live in a society that has trained us to work against each other."

Lesson 5
Struggles always take us back to the land

> This land hunger – this absolutely fundamental and essential thing to any real emancipation of the slaves – was continually pushed by all emancipated Negroes and their representatives in every Southern state. It was met by ridicule, by anger, and by dishonest and insincere efforts to satisfy it apparently (Du Bois 1935, 601).

Abolition is deeply agrarian, though agrifood scholars have been slow to link prisons and food systems. Historians trace ideological and material roots back to the plantation, a system which grew not only cotton but a hierarchical workplace management that, argues Desmond (2019), gave rise to a "uniquely severe and unbridled" form of US capitalism. Long before industrial assembly (and meatpacking disassembly) lines, the plantation enacted punishing data-tracking systems to capitalize on economies of scale in cotton farming. Overseers meticulously controlled worker line speeds, recording daily picking quotas, and disciplined underperformers. "Each individual having a stated number of pounds of cotton to pick," Henry Watson, a formerly enslaved worker, wrote in 1848, "the deficit of which was made up by as many lashes being applied to the poor slave's back" (quoted in Desmond 2019). This approach worked. By 1862, the average enslaved field worker was picking about 400 percent as much cotton as his or her counterpart in 1801.

After the Civil War, planters turned to convict leasing to keep this system intact, despite legal emancipation. Though convict leasing was gradually phased out during the early twentieth century in most states, slave labor continues to service prison farms in the twenty-first century (Evans 2018). Former plantations make up some of the 130,000 agricultural acres currently maintained and operated by the Texas Department of Criminal Justice (Reese and Carr 2020). The Angola state penitentiary remains a working plantation, with inmates growing food for all of Louisiana's prisons and cattle for the open market. "The prisoners do the farming under the supervision of shot-gun carrying guards on horseback" (Goldberg 2015).

Gilmore describes the expansion of prisons in California as "a geographical solution to socio-economic problems" (1999, 174), showing how California's prisons like San Quentin were sited on devalued rural land, most, in fact, on formerly irrigated agricultural acres. Extending this argument in *Golden Gulag* (2007), she situates the prison-industrial complex within historical cycles of global capital accumulation that have continuously required and therefore reproduced a carceral system to secure and mobilize surplus land, labor, finance capital, and state power. Penitentiaries and detention centers are stolen landscapes, mutually constituted by Indigenous dispossession, border imperialism, and racial capitalism.

Land therefore shares a cradle with abolition. What W.E.B. Du Bois (1935, 601) called "land hunger" among freedmen during Reconstruction enabled two generations of Black workers to eke out survival on the land through the early twentieth century. But in the decades since World War II, massive dispossession nearly destroyed Black agriculture. Black farmers in the USA peaked in 1920, when they numbered nearly 1 million. Today, of the country's 3.4 million total farmers, only 1.4 percent are Black, according to USDA census data (USDA 2019). Black families today tend a scant 4.7 million acres – a nearly 90 percent loss since 1920. This land "loss" is perhaps better described as a land grab, as Black families' land was recaptured by white landowners through a variety of legal mechanisms – including tax sales, partition sales, and foreclosures – as well as illegal mechanisms such as swindling by lawyers and speculators, and outright acts of violence or intimidation (Newkirk 2019).

In recent years, however, as Black agrarianism makes a comeback in communities both urban and rural (Snipstal 2015; White 2018), new attention has turned to reparations (NBJFA 2020). When co-founder Leah Penniman started Soul Fire Farms in 2011, her goal was building a multi-racial, sustainable farming organization that would run food sovereignty programs, offer training to Black and Brown farmers, and support activist retreats (Collier 2018). In February 2018, Soul Fire also began leading a movement of Black farmers calling for reparations for centuries of slavery and racial inequity in the US. Central to this effort is a Reparations Map for Black and Indigenous Farmers (Soul Fire 2018), which as of spring 2020, included 114 organizations around the country led by farmers of color. The map details farmers in need of land, resources, and funding, and aims to connect them with organizations, foundations, and individual donors to support their work. Other BIPOC-led organizations working specifically on reparations include the Northeast Farmers of Color Land Trust and the Black Farmer Fund, a fund that pools money from investors to provide non-extractive loans to Black-owned farming and food businesses (Penniman 2019). At the national scale, reparations efforts are coordinated by the National Black Food and Justice Alliance, a group representing 21 farmer organizations including Cooperation Jackson, the Southeastern African American Farmers' Organic Network, and the Black Dirt Farm Collective, among others.

Agroecologists have much to learn from Black agrarians, including from their legacy of sustainable agriculture: the enslaved West African women who carried their indigenous rice systems from the Senegambian region to the early-US Carolinas (Carney 2001); men like George Washington Carver who, though often remembered as a peanut farmer, presciently advocated for legume-based polyculture, composting, and dumpster diving (White 2018). In turn, agroecology may have something to offer BIPOC communities in their efforts not just to take back the land – but to remain on it.

5

Conclusion

In this paper, I have argued that COVID-19 hardly initiated but helped reveal systematic oppressions of communities of color and the poor through their connections to agriculture and food. Racial capitalism long ago began carving grooves that pathogens now readily exploit: from tropical landscapes where agribusiness-driven deforestation and monoculture cropping are setting once-contained viruses free, to CAFOs[1] where pathogens incubate and spread with now-regular frequency; from food banks and food pantries unable to keep up with surging demand for basic needs, to the livelihood trap facing poor, Black, and Brown communities, whose labor is considered essential but whose lives, evidently, are not.

One way of thinking about these interconnected crises is through the lens of the metabolic rift, which considers how historical cycles of accumulation have separated humans from agrarian landscapes, plants from livestock, and communities from working knowledge of their own agriculture. Agroecology offers a way to heal this rift, ecologically, socially, and epistemically, and many precedents have been set for this work. Ecologically, communities can deploy farming practices to enhance nature's matrix. Diversification at farm, field, and landscape levels not only will reconstitute synergies among biodiversity, agriculture, and food sovereignty but also will buffer against new viral spillovers. Socially and epis-

---

1.   Concentrated Animal Feeding Operations

temically, structural racism and racial capitalism demand more active, reflexive, and committed attention from agroecologists if they seek transformation over reform. Mass anti-police protests amidst COVID-19 revived a clear, uncompromising discourse of abolition that agroecologists can learn from and support.

Abolitionists teach that in order to have a world with, you must create a world *without* – a watchword for agroecologists attempting to "scale out" within and against a massive legal, institutional, material, and financial apparatus of the current global food economy. As abolitionists demonstrate, reform proposals molt into increasingly cunning and sophisticated guises, which are bound to split agroecologists' ranks unless they understand the strategy for what it is. Abolitionists embrace revolutionary change by reminding us that there is nothing normal, natural, or unchangeable about the social institutions that society has erected. From slavery to Jim Crow, the once "everlasting suns" are closer to stardust now. Can we imagine, then, a world without prison industrial complexes, agroindustrial complexes, and other strongholds of racial capitalism? Abolitionists underline that abolish is a *verb*, a crucial recognition that gets us past an abolitionist/agroecologist identity binary to where we can think materially and practically about "abolitionist agroecology" and "agroecological abolition." Land reparations will constitute an important site of abolitionist-agroecology work, as will advancing biodiversity-based practices and horizontal learning to keep territories in communities' hands long term. The conjuncture of COVID-19 and systemic racism has created an extraordinary moment for abolitionist agroecology, should we choose to take it.

Bibliography

8toAbolition. 2020. "#8toAbolition." https://www.8toabolition.com. [Google Scholar]

Akuno, K. 2020. "May Day People's Strike! Target, Amazon, Instacart Workers Demand Safe Conditions & Pandemic Relief," Interview with Kali Akuno. *Democracy Now!*. [Google Scholar]

Altieri, M. A. 1995. *Agroecology: The Science of Sustainable Agriculture.* Boulder, CO: Westview Press. [Google Scholar]

Altieri, M. A., and C. I. Nicholls. 2020. "Agroecology and the Reconstruction of a Post-COVID-19 Agriculture." *The Journal of Peasant Studies*, July, 1–18. doi:10.1080/03066150.2020.1782891. [Taylor & Francis Online], [Web of Science®], [Google Scholar]

Altieri, M. A., and V. M. Toledo. 2011. "The Agroecological Revolution in Latin America: Rescuing Nature, Ensuring Food Sovereignty and Empowering Peasants." *Journal of Peasant Studies* 38 (3): 587–612. doi:10.1080/03066150.2011.582947. [Taylor & Francis Online], [Web of Science®], [Google Scholar]

Álvarez Febles, N., and G. F. Félix. 2020. "Hurricane María, Agroecology and Climate Change Resiliency." In *Climate Justice and Community Renewal: Resistance and Grassroots Solutions*, edited by B. Tokar, and T. Gilbertson, 1–14. New York, NY: Routledge (pre-print). doi:10.4324/9780429277146. [Crossref], [Google Scholar]

Anderson, C. R., J. Bruil, M. J. Chappell, C. Kiss, and M. P. Pimbert. 2019. "From Transition to Domains of Transformation: Getting to Sustainable and Just Food Systems through Agroecology." *Sustainability* 11 (19): 5272. doi:10.3390/su11195272. [Crossref], [Web of Science®], [Google Scholar]

Bezner Kerr, R., P. R. Berti, and L. Shumba. 2011. "Effects of a Participatory Agriculture and Nutrition Education Project on Child Growth in Northern Malawi." *Public Health Nutrition* 14 (8): 1466–1472. doi:10.1017/S1368980010002545. [Crossref], [PubMed], [Web of Science®], [Google Scholar]

Bezner Kerr, R., C. Hickey, E. Lupafya, and L. Dakishoni. 2019. "Repairing Rifts or Reproducing Inequalities? Agroecology, Food Sovereignty, and Gender Justice in Malawi." *The Journal of Peasant Studies* 46 (7): 1499–1518. doi:10.1080/03066150.2018.1547897. [Taylor & Francis Online], [Web of Science®], [Google Scholar]

Brent, Z. W., C. M. Schiavoni, and A. Alonso-Fradejas. 2015. "Contextualising Food Sovereignty: The Politics of Convergence among Movements in the USA." *Third World Quarterly* 36 (3): 618–635. doi:10.1080/01436597.2015.1023570. [Taylor & Francis Online], [Web of Science®], [Google Scholar]

Brescia, S., ed. 2017. *Fertile Ground: Scaling Agroecology from the Ground Up*. Oakland, CA: Food First Books. [Google Scholar]

Buttel, F. H. 2005. "Ever Since Hightower: The Politics of Agricultural Research Activism in the Molecular Age." *Agriculture and Human Values* 22 (3): 275–283. doi:10.1007/s10460-005-6043-3. [Crossref], [Web of Science®], [Google Scholar]

Calderón, C. I., C. Jerónimo, A. Praun, J. Reyna, D. Santos Castillo, R. León, R. Hogan, and J. P. Prado Córdova. 2018. "Agroecology-based Farming Provides Grounds for More Resilient Livelihoods among Smallholders in Western Guatemala." *Agroecology and Sustainable Food Systems* 42 (10): 1128–1169. doi:10.1080/21683565.2018.1489933. [Taylor & Francis Online], [Web of Science®], [Google Scholar]

Carney, J. A. 2001. *Black Rice: The African Origins of Rice Cultivation in the Americas*. Cambridge, MA: Harvard University Press. [Google Scholar]

Center for Popular Democracy. 2020. "Congress Must Divest the Billion Dollar Police Budget and Invest in Public Education." *The Center for Popular Democracy*, June 10. [Google Scholar]

Chang, V. L., and S. M. Holmes. 2020. "US Food Workers Are in Danger. That Threatens All of Us." *The Guardian*, April 14. [Google Scholar]

Chappell, M. J. 2018. *Beginning to End Hunger: Food and the Environment in Belo Horizonte, Brazil, and Beyond*. Oakland: University of California Press. [Crossref], [Google Scholar]

Clark, B., and J. B. Foster. 2009. "Ecological Imperialism and the Global Metabolic Rift: Unequal Exchange and the Guano/Nitrates Trade." *International Journal of Comparative Sociology* 50 (3–4): 311–334. doi:10.1177/0020715209105144. [Crossref], [Web of Science®], [Google Scholar]

Clausen, R. 2007. "Healing the Rift." *Monthly Review*, May 1. [Google Scholar]

COC. 2020. "Cops Off Campus: A Statement of Black Solidarity." September. https://bit.ly/3pEE5j5. [Google Scholar]

Collier, A. K. 2018. "A Reparations Map for Farmers of Color May Help Right Historical Wrongs." *Civil Eats*, June 4. [Google Scholar]

Cook, C. D. 2020. "Get Ready for Mass Strikes Across the US this May Day." *In These Times*, April 30. [Google Scholar]

CPD (The Center for Popular Democracy). 2020. "Congress Must Divest the Billion Dollar Police Budget and Invest in Public Education." *The Center for Popular Democracy*, June 10. [Google Scholar]

CR (Critical Resistance). 2012. "Abolitionist Toolkit, Part 4: Common Sense, Frequently Asked Questions, Tools for Framing Abolitionist Arguments in Terms of What We Want." http://criticalresistance.org/wp-content/uploads/2012/06/Ab-Toolkit-Part-4.pdf. [Google Scholar]

CR (Critical Resistance). 2020. "What is the PIC? What is Abolition?" http://criticalresistance.org/about/not-so-common-language/. [Google Scholar]

Crampton, L. 2020. "Meat Shortages Loom due to Plant Closures." *POLITICO: Morning Agriculture*. [Google Scholar]

CRDT (COVID Racial Data Tracker). 2020. "The COVID Racial Data Tracker." *The COVID Tracking Project*. https://covidtracking.com/race. [Google Scholar]

Cronon, W. 1991. *Nature's Metropolis: Chicago and the Great West*. New York: WW Norton & Company. [Google Scholar]

Dagang, A. B. K., and P. K. R. Nair. 2003. "Silvopastoral Research and Adoption in Central America: Recent Findings and Recommendations for Future Directions." *Agroforestry Systems* 59 (2): 149–155. doi:10.1023/A:1026394019808. [Crossref], [Web of Science®], [Google Scholar]

Daszak, P. 2020. "'Pure Baloney': Zoologist Debunks Trump's COVID-19 Origin Theory, Explains Animal-Human Transmission." Interview with Peter Daszak. *Democracy Now!*. [Google Scholar]

Davis, M. 1995. "Hell Factories in the Field: A Prison-Industrial Complex." *The Nation* 260 (7): 229–233. [Web of Science®], [Google Scholar]

Davis, A. Y. 2003. *Are Prisons Obsolete? Open Media Book.* New York: Seven Stories Press. [Google Scholar]

Davis, M. 2020. "Mike Davis on COVID-19: The Monster is at the Door." *Haymarketbooks.org*, March 12. [Google Scholar]

DeLonge, M. S., A. Miles, and L. Carlisle. 2016. "Investing in the Transition to Sustainable Agriculture." *Environmental Science & Policy* 55: 266–273. doi:10.1016/j.envsci.2015.09.013. [Crossref], [Web of Science®], [Google Scholar]

de Molina, M. G., P. Petersen, F. Garrido Peña, and F. R. Caporal. 2020. *Political Agroecology: Advancing the Transition to Sustainable Food Systems.* Boca Raton, FL: CRC Press. [Google Scholar]

Desmond, M. 2019. "American Capitalism is Brutal. You can Trace that to the Plantation." *The New York Times Magazine*, August 14. [Google Scholar]

Du Bois, W. E. B. 1935. *Black Reconstruction in America: Toward a History of the Part of Which Black Folk Played in the Attempt to Reconstruct Democracy in America, 1860–1880.* New Brunswick, NJ: Transaction Publishers. [Google Scholar]

DuPuis, E. M., E. Ransom, and M. R. Worosz. 2020. "Why Farmers are Dumping Milk Down the Drain and Letting Produce Rot in Fields." *The Conversation*, April 23. [Google Scholar]

DuVernay, A. 2016. *13th.* Sherman Oaks, CA: Netflix Original Documentary, Kandoo Films. [Google Scholar]

Edelman, M. 2014. Food sovereignty: forgotten genealogies and future regulatory challenges, *The Journal of Peasant Studies*, 41:6, 959-978, DOI: 10.1080/03066150.2013.876998

EPI (Economic Policy Institute). 2020. "Not Everybody can Work from Home: Black and Hispanic Workers are Much Less Likely to be Able to Telework." *Economic Policy Institute*, March 19. https://www.epi.org/blog/black-and-hispanic-workers-are-much-less-likely-to-be-able-to-work-from-home/. [Google Scholar]

Eskenazi, B., P. Moreno, and A. Voit. 2020. "We Must Assure the Health of Farmworkers." *Monterey Herald*, March 28. https://www.montereyherald.com/guest-opinion-we-must-assure-the-health-of-farmworkers. [Google Scholar]

Evans, S. 2018. "Is Prison Labor the Future of Our Food System?" *Food First*. September 7. https://foodfirst.org/is-prison-labor-the-future-of-our-food-system/. [Google Scholar]

Fairbairn, Madeleine. 2010. "Framing Resistance: International Food Regimes & the Roots of Food Sovereignty." In *Food Sovereignty: Reconnecting Food, Nature and Community*, edited by Hannah Wittman, Annette A. Desmarais, and Wiebe, Nettie, 15–32. Oakland: Food First Books.

FAO, IFAD, UNICEF, WFP, and WHO. 2020. *The State of Food Security and Nutrition in the World 2020: Transforming Food Systems for Affordable Healthy Diets*. Rome: FAO. doi:10.4060/ca9692en. [Crossref], [Google Scholar]

Fearnley, L. 2015. "Wild Goose Chase: The Displacement of Influenza Research in the Fields of Poyang Lake, China." *Cultural Anthropology* 30 (1): 12–35. doi:10.14506/ca30.1.03. [Crossref], [Web of Science®], [Google Scholar]

Fisher, D., and D. Heymann. 2020. "Q&A: The Novel Coronavirus Outbreak Causing COVID-19." *BMC Medicine* 18 (1): 57. doi:10.1186/s12916-020-01533-w. [Crossref], [PubMed], [Web of Science®], [Google Scholar]

Food & Environment Reporting Network. 2020. "Mapping Covid-19 Outbreaks in the Food System." Updated November 30. https://thefern.org/2020/04/mapping-covid-19-in-meat-and-food-processing-plants/. [Google Scholar]

Foster, J. B. 1999. "Marx's Theory of Metabolic Rift: Classical Foundations for Environmental Sociology." *American Journal of Sociology* 105 (2): 366–405. doi:10.1086/210315. [Crossref], [Web of Science®], [Google Scholar]

Foster, J. B., and F. Magdoff. 2000. "Liebig, Marx, and the Depletion of Soil Fertility: Relevance for Today's Agriculture." In *Hungry for Profit: The Agribusiness Threat to Farmers, Food, and the Environment*, edited by F. Magdoff, J. B. Foster, and F. H. Buttel, 43–60. New York: Monthly Review Press. [Google Scholar]

Garbach, K., M. Lubell, and F. A. J. DeClerck. 2012. "Payment for Ecosystem Services: The Roles of Positive Incentives and Information Sharing in Stimulating Adoption of Silvopastoral Conservation Practices." *Agriculture, Ecosystems & Environment* 156: 27–36. doi:10.1016/j.agee.2012.04.017. [Crossref], [Web of Science®], [Google Scholar]

Gies, H. 2018. "Agroecology as a Tool of Sovereignty and Resilience in Puerto Rico after Hurricane Maria." *Civil Eats*, October 19. [Google Scholar]

Gilbert, M., X. Xiao, and T. P. Robinson. 2017. "Intensifying Poultry Production Systems and the Emergence of Avian Influenza in China: A 'One Health/Ecohealth' Epitome." *Archives of Public Health* 75 (1): 48. doi:10.1186/s13690-017-0218-4. [Crossref], [PubMed], [Google Scholar]

Gilmore, R. W. 1999. "Globalisation and US Prison Growth: From Military Keynesianism to Post-Keynesian Militarism." *Race & Class* 40 (2–3): 171–188.

doi:10.1177/030639689904000212. [Crossref], [Web of Science®], [Google Scholar]

Gilmore, R. W. 2007. *Golden Gulag: Prisons, Surplus, Crisis, and Opposition in Globalizing California*. Berkeley: University of California Press. [Crossref], [Google Scholar]

Gilmore, R. W. 2020. "Geographies of Racial Capitalism with Ruth Wilson Gilmore – An Antipode Foundation Film." https://youtu.be/2CS627aKrJI. [Google Scholar]

Giraldo, O. F., and N. McCune. 2019. "Can the State Take Agroecology to Scale? Public Policy Experiences in Agroecological Territorialization from Latin America." *Agroecology and Sustainable Food Systems* 43 (7–8): 785–809. doi:10.1080/21683565.2019.1585402. [Taylor & Francis Online], [Web of Science®], [Google Scholar]

Giraldo, O. F., and P. M. Rosset. 2018. "Agroecology as a Territory in Dispute: Between Institutionality and Social Movements." *The Journal of Peasant Studies* 45 (3): 545–564. doi:10.1080/03066150.2017.1353496. [Taylor & Francis Online], [Web of Science®], [Google Scholar]

Gliessman, S. R. 2015. *Agroecology: The Ecology of Sustainable Food Systems*. 3rd ed. Boca Raton, FL: CRC Press/Taylor & Francis Group. [Google Scholar]

Gobbi, J. 2002. *Enfoques silvopastoriles integrados para el manejo de ecosistemas en Colombia, Costa Rica y Nicaragua: Análisis económico-financiero ex-ante de la inversión en los SSP propuestos para cada país*. [Google Scholar]

Goldberg, J. 2015. "A Matter of Black Lives." *The Atlantic*, September. [Google Scholar]

Grabell, M., C. Perlman, and B. Yeung. 2020. "Emails Reveal Chaos as Meatpacking Companies Fought Health Agencies Over COVID-19 Outbreaks in their Plants." *ProPublica*, June 12. [Google Scholar]

Greger, M. 2020. *How to Survive a Pandemic*. New York: Flatiron Books. [Google Scholar]

Haedicke, M. 2020. "To Understand the Danger of COVID-19 Outbreaks in Meatpacking Plants, Look at the Industry's History." *The Conversation*, May 6. [Google Scholar]

Haley, S. 2016. *No Mercy Here: Gender, Punishment, and the Making of Jim Crow Modernity*. Justice, Power, and Politics. Chapel Hill: The University of North Carolina Press. [Crossref], [Google Scholar]

Hamer, F. L. 1964. "Testimony Before the Credential Committee," Democratic National Convention, delivered August 22, 1964. [Google Scholar]

Hanski, I., and D. Simberloff. 1997. "The Metapopulation Approach, Its History, Conceptual Domain, and Application to Conservation." In *Metapopulation Biology*, edited by I. Hanski, and M. E. Gilpin, 5–26. Elsevier. doi:10.1016/B978-012323445-2/50003-1. [Crossref], [Google Scholar]

Harvey, D. 2020. "Anti-Capitalist Politics in the Time of COVID-19." *Jacobin*. [Google Scholar]

Healy, J. 2020. "Workers Fearful of the Coronavirus are Getting Fired and Losing their Benefits." *The New York Times*, June 4. [Google Scholar]

Heffernan, W. 2000. "Concentration of Ownership and Control in Agriculture." In *Hungry for Profit: The Agribusiness Threat to Farmers, Food, and the Environment*, edited by F. Magdoff, J. B. Foster, and F. H. Buttel, 61–76. New York: Monthly Review Press. [Google Scholar]

Hendrickson, M. K. 2015. "Resilience in a Concentrated and Consolidated Food System." *Journal of Environmental Studies and Sciences* 5 (3): 418–431. doi:10.1007/s13412-015-0292-2. [Crossref], [Google Scholar]

Herskind, M. 2019. "Some Reflections on Prison Abolition"." *Medium*, December 7. [Google Scholar]

HLPE (High Level Panel of Experts). 2019. "Agroecological Approaches and Other Innovations for Sustainable Agriculture and Food Systems that Enhance Food Security and Nutrition.' A Report by the High Level Panel of Experts on Food Security and Nutrition of the Committee on World Food Security, Rome. http://www.fao.org/3/ca5602en/ca5602en.pdf. [Google Scholar]

Holmes, S. M. 2013. *Fresh Fruit, Broken Bodies: Migrant Farmworkers in the United States*. Berkeley: University of California Press. [Crossref], [Google Scholar]

Holt Giménez, E., and A. Shattuck. 2011. "Food Crises, Food Regimes and Food Movements: Rumblings of Reform or Tides of Transformation?" *Journal of Peasant Studies* 38 (1): 109–144. doi:10.1080/03066150.2010.538578. [Taylor & Francis Online], [Web of Science®], [Google Scholar]

Howard, P. H. 2016. *Concentration and Power in the Food System: Who Controls What We Eat?* New York: Bloomsbury. [Crossref], [Google Scholar]

Howard, P. H. 2017. "Consolidation in Global Meat Processing." https://phil-howard.net/2017/06/21/consolidation-in-global-meat-processing/. [Google Scholar]

Huang, C., Y. Wang, X. Li, L. Ren, J. Zhao, Y.Hu, L. Zhang, et al. 2020. "Clinical Features of Patients Infected with 2019 Novel Coronavirus in Wuhan, China." *The Lancet* 395 (10223): 497–506. doi:10.1016/S0140-6736(20)30183-5. [Crossref], [PubMed], [Web of Science®], [Google Scholar]

Hui, D. S., E. I. Azhar, T. A. Madani, F. Ntoumi, R. Kock, O. Dar, G. Ippolito, et al. 2020. "The Continuing 2019-NCoV Epidemic Threat of Novel Coronaviruses to Global Health – The Latest 2019 Novel Coronavirus Outbreak in Wuhan, China." *International Journal of Infectious Diseases* 91 (February): 264–266. doi:10.1016/j.ijid.2020.01.009. [Crossref], [PubMed], [Google Scholar]

IAASTD. 2009. *International Assessment of Agricultural Knowledge, Science and Technology for Development: Global Report.* Edited by B. McIntyre, H. R. Herren, J. Wakhungu, and R. T. Watson. Washington, DC: Island Press. [Google Scholar]

IATP and GRAIN. 2018. "Emissions Impossible: How Big Meat and Dairy are Heating Up the Planet." https://www.iatp.org/emissions-impossible. [Google Scholar]

Illing, S. 2020. "The 'Abolish the Police' Movement, Explained by 7 Scholars and Activists." *Vox*, June 12. [Google Scholar]

Immerwahr, D. 2019. *How to Hide an Empire: A History of the Greater United States.* New York: Farrar, Straus and Giroux. [Google Scholar]

IPES-Food. 2016. "From Uniformity to Diversity: A paradigm shift from industrial agriculture to diversified agroecological systems." International Panel of Experts on Sustainable Food systems. [Crossref], [Google Scholar]

Jadhav, R. 2020. "Indian Farmers Feed Strawberries to Cattle as Lockdown Hits Transport." *Reuters*, April 2. [Google Scholar]

Jayaraman, S. 2013. *Behind the Kitchen Door.* Ithaca: Cornell University Press. [Google Scholar]

JHU (Johns Hopkins University). 2020. "COVID-19 Map." *Johns Hopkins Coronavirus Resource Center.* https://coronavirus.jhu.edu/map.html. [Google Scholar]

Johnson, M. 2020. "States Tell Workers They'll Lose Unemployment Benefits If They Refuse to Return to Jobs." *The Hill*, April 28. [Google Scholar]

Johnson, G. T., and A.Lubin, eds. 2017. *Futures of Black Radicalism.* New York City: Verso. [Google Scholar]

Kaba, M. 2020. "Yes, We Mean Literally Abolish the Police." *The New York Times*, June 12. [Google Scholar]

Kandel, W., and E. A. Parrado. 2005. "Restructuring of the US Meat Processing Industry and New Hispanic Migrant Destinations." *Population and Development Review* 31 (3): 447–471. doi:10.1111/j.1728-4457.2005.00079.x. [Crossref], [Web of Science®], [Google Scholar]

Kelley, R. D. G. 2017. "What did Cedric Robinson Mean by Racial Capitalism?" Text. *Boston Review*, January 12. [Google Scholar]

Kelley, R. D. G. 2020. "Historian Robin D.G. Kelley: Years of Racial Justice Organizing Laid Groundwork for Today's Uprising." *Democracy Now!* June 11. [Google Scholar]

Kremen, C., and A. Miles. 2012. "Ecosystem Services in Biologically Diversified versus Conventional Farming Systems: Benefits, Externalities, and Trade-Offs." *Ecology and Society* 17 (4). doi:10.5751/ES-05035-170440. [Crossref], [Web of Science®], [Google Scholar]

Lappé, F.M., and J. Collins. 1986. *World Hunger: Twelve Myths.* New York, NY: Grove Press.

Latinne, A., B.Hu, K. J. Olival, G. Zhu, L. Zhang, H. Li, A. A. Chmura, et al. 2020. "Origin and Cross-species Transmission of Bat Coronaviruses in China." BioRxiv preprint: *Evolutionary Biology*. doi:10.1101/2020.05.31.116061. [Crossref], [PubMed], [Google Scholar]

Levins, R. 1969. Some demographic and genetic consequences of environmental heterogeneity for biological control. *American Entomologist*, 15(3): 237-240.

LFGP (List of George Floyd Protests). 2020. "List of George Floyd Protests Outside the United States." *Wikipedia.* [Google Scholar]

Lucas, A. 2020. "Meatpacking Union Says 25% of US Pork Production Hit by Coronavirus Closures." *CNBC.* April 23. https://www.cnbc.com/2020/04/23/meatpacking-union-says-25percent-of-us-pork-production-hit-by-coronavirus-closures.html. [Google Scholar]

Lynteris, C., and L. Fearnley. 2020. "Why Shutting Down Chinese 'Wet Markets' Could be a Terrible Mistake." *The Conversation*, January 31. [Google Scholar]

M4BL (Movement for Black Lives). 2020a. "Defund Toolkit: Concrete Steps toward Divestment from Policing & Investment in Community Safety." *Defund Toolkit.* https://bit.ly/3pzn7Cw. [Google Scholar]

M4BL (Movement for Black Lives). 2020b. "Week of Action: TUESDAY – Invest/ Divest." June. https://m4bl.org/week-of-action/tuesday/. [Google Scholar]

MADR (Mutual Aid Disaster Relief). 2020. "When Every Community is Ground Zero: Pulling Each Other Through a Pandemic." March 14. https://mutualaiddisasterrelief.org/when-every-community-is-ground-zero-pulling-each-other-through-a-pandemic/. [Google Scholar]

Mandel, E. 1970. *An introduction to Marxist economic thought*. New York: Pathfinder, p. 52.

Martínez-Torres, M.E., and P.M. Rosset. 2010. "La Vía Campesina: The Birth and Evolution of a Transnational Social Movement." *The Journal of Peasant Studies* 37 (1): 149–75. doi:10.1080/03066150903498804.

Martínez-Torres, M.E., and P.M. Rosset. 2014. "*Diálogo de Saberes* in La Vía Campesina: Food Sovereignty and Agroecology." *The Journal of Peasant Studies* 41 (6): 979–997. [Taylor & Francis Online], [Web of Science®], [Google Scholar]

Marx, K. 1981. *Capital, Volume 3*. New York: Vintage. [Google Scholar]

Mayer, J. 2020. "How Trump is Helping Tycoons Exploit the Pandemic." *The New Yorker*, July 20. [Google Scholar]

McCarty, E. 2020. "Yakima County Farmworkers Called 'Sacrificial Lambs' of Pandemic." *Crosscut*, June 29. [Google Scholar]

Mandel, E. *An Introduction to Marxist Economic Thought* (New York: Pathfinder, 1970), p. 52

Méndez, V. E., C. M. Bacon, R. Cohen, and S. R. Gliessman, eds. 2016. *Agroecology: A Transdisciplinary, Participatory and Action-oriented Approach*. Boca Raton: CRC Press. [Google Scholar]

Meyersohn, N. 2020. "Black Grocery Workers Feel Increasingly Vulnerable to Coronavirus." *CNN*, April 15. [Google Scholar]

Mier y Terán Giménez Cacho, M., O. F. Giraldo, M. Aldasoro, H. Morales, B. G. Ferguson, P. Rosset, A. Khadse, and C. Campos. 2018. "Bringing Agroecology to Scale: Key Drivers and Emblematic Cases." *Agroecology and Sustainable Food Systems* 42 (6): 637–665. doi:10.1080/21683565.2018.1443313. [Taylor & Francis Online], [Web of Science®], [Google Scholar]

Mitchell, T. J. 2020. "Smithfield Foods Employee Tests Positive for Coronavirus." *Argus Leader*, March 26. [Google Scholar]

Moore, J. W. 2000. "Environmental Crises and the Metabolic Rift in World-historical Perspective." *Organization & Environment* 13 (2): 123–157. doi:10.1177/1086026600132001. [Crossref], [Google Scholar]

MPD150. 2020. "What are We Talking about When We Talk about 'a Police-free Future?'" June 10. http://www.mpd150.com/what-are-we-talking-about-when-we-talk-about-a-police-free-future/. [Crossref], [Google Scholar]

Mulvany, L., J. Skerritt, P. Mosendz, and J. Attwood. 2020. "Scared and Sick, US Meat Workers Crowd into Reopened Plants." *Bloomberg News*, May 21. [Google Scholar]

Myers, S. L. 2020. "China's Omnivorous Markets are in the Eye of a Lethal Outbreak Once Again." *The New York Times*, January 25. [Google Scholar]

National Academies of Sciences, Engineering, and Medicine. 2005. *'The Threat of Pandemic Influenza: Are We Ready?' Workshop Summary*. Washington, DC: National Academies Press. doi:10.17226/11150. [Crossref], [Google Scholar]

NBJFA (National Black Food & Justice Alliance). 2020. "Modes of Focus: Land Liberation." https://www.blackfoodjustice.org. [Google Scholar]

Nelson, K. A., and C. Marston. 2020. "Refugee Migration Histories in a Meatpacking Town: Blurring the Line between Primary and Secondary Migration." *Journal of International Migration and Integration* 21 (1): 77–91. doi:10.1007/s12134-019-00694-9. [Crossref], [Web of Science®], [Google Scholar]

Nelson, M. I., C. Viboud, A. L. Vincent, M. R. Culhane, S. E. Detmer, D. E. Wentworth, A. Rambaut, M. A. Suchard, E. C. Holmes, and P. Lemey. 2015. "Global Migration of Influenza A Viruses in Swine." *Nature Communications* 6 (1): 6696. doi:10.1038/ncomms7696. [Crossref], [PubMed], [Google Scholar]

Newkirk, V. R. 2019. "The Great Land Robbery." *The Atlantic*, September. [Google Scholar]

Nicholls, C. I., and M. A. Altieri. 2018. "Pathways for the Amplification of Agroecology." *Agroecology and Sustainable Food Systems* 42 (10): 1170–1193. doi:10.1080/21683565.2018.1499578. [Taylor & Francis Online], [Web of Science®], [Google Scholar]

Nylen, L., and L. Crampton. 2020. "'Something isn't Right': US Probes Soaring Beef Prices." *Politico*, May 25. [Google Scholar]

Nyéléni 2007. "Declaration of Nyéléni – Via Campesina – Newsletter, Bulletin, Boletin." Sélingué, Mali. https://nyeleni.org/spip.php?article290.

NYT (New York Times). 2020. "Why is OSHA AWOL?" *The New York Times Editorial Board*, June 21. https://www.nytimes.com/2020/06/21/opinion/coronavirus-osha-work-safety.html. [Google Scholar]

Oppel, R. A., R. Gebeloff, K. K. R. Lai, W. Wright, and M. Smith. 2020. "The Fullest Look Yet at the Racial Inequity of Coronavirus." *The New York Times*, July 5. [Google Scholar]

OSHA (Occupational Health and Safety Administration). 2020. "Statement of Enforcement Policy Regarding Meat and Poultry Processing Facilities."

United States Department of Labor, April 28. https://www.dol.gov/news-room/releases/osha/osha20200428-1. [Google Scholar]

PAeP (People's Agroecology Process). 2020a. "The People's Agroecology Process: Unlocking Our Power through Agroecology." June. https://whyhunger.org/wp-content/uploads/2020/06/1132-People-Agroecology_ENGLISH_ONLINE-Single.pdf. [Google Scholar]

PAeP (People's Agroecology Process). 2020b. "The People's Agroecology Process: Webinar." June 24. [Google Scholar]

Pagiola, S., E. Ramírez, J. Gobbi, C. de Haan, M. Ibrahim, E. Murgueitio, and J. P. Ruíz. 2007. "Paying for the Environmental Services of Silvopastoral Practices in Nicaragua." *Ecological Economics* 64 (2): 374–385. doi:10.1016/j.ecolecon.2007.04.014. [Crossref], [Web of Science®], [Google Scholar]

Patel, R. 2009. "Food Sovereignty." *The Journal of Peasant Studies* 36 (3): 663–706. doi:10.1080/03066150903143079.

Penniman, L. 2019. "A New Generation of Black Farmers is Returning to the Land." *Yes! Magazine*, November 19. https://www.yesmagazine.org/social-justice/2019/11/19/land-black-farmers-reparations. [Google Scholar]

Perfecto, I., J. H. Vandermeer, and A. L. Wright. 2009. *Nature's Matrix: Linking Agriculture, Conservation and Food Sovereignty.* London; Sterling, VA: Earthscan. [Crossref], [Google Scholar]

Pershan, C. 2020. "Restaurant and Bar Employees Make Up 60 Percent of Jobs Lost in March." *Eater*, April 6. [Google Scholar]

Pew. 2009. "A Portrait of Unauthorized Immigrants in the United States." *Pew Research Center's Hispanic Trends Project.* https://www.pewresearch.org/wp-content/uploads/sites/5/reports/107.pdf. [Google Scholar]

Pfannenstiel, B. 2020. "Iowa Officials Won't Disclose Coronavirus Outbreaks at Meatpacking Plants Unless Media Asks." *Des Moines Register*, May 27. [Google Scholar]

Philpott, T. 2009. "Symptom: Swine Flu. Diagnosis: Industrial Agriculture?" *Grist*, April 29. [Google Scholar]

Pimbert, M. 2015. "Agroecology as an Alternative Vision to Conventional Development and Climate-Smart Agriculture." *Development* 58 (2): 286–298. doi:10.1057/s41301-016-0013-5. [Crossref], [Google Scholar]

PPI (Prison Policy Initiative). 2020. "Mass Incarceration: The Whole Pie 2020." March 24. https://www.prisonpolicy.org/reports/pie2020.html. [Google Scholar]

Proctor, C. 2020. "As Businesses Prepare to Reopen, Workers Weigh COVID-19 Risk against the Need for a Paycheck." *The Texas Tribune*, April 28. [Google Scholar]

Reese, A., and R. Carr. 2020. "Overthrowing the Food System's Plantation Paradigm." *Civil Eats*, June 19. [Google Scholar]

Rigueiro-Rodríguez, A., J. McAdam, and M. R. Mosquera-Losada. 2008. *Agroforestry in Europe: Current Status and Future Prospects*. Netherlands: Springer. [Google Scholar]

Rios, E. 2020. "How Black Oaklanders Finally Expelled the School Police." *Mother Jones*, November/December. [Google Scholar]

Robbins, P. 2011. *Political Ecology: A Critical Introduction*. 2nd ed. Malden: J. Wiley & Sons. [Google Scholar]

Robbins, J. 2012. "The Ecology of Disease." *The New York Times*, July 14. https://www.nytimes.com/2012/07/15/sunday-review/the-ecology-of-disease.html. [Google Scholar]

Robinson, C. 1983. *Black Marxism: The Making of the Black Radical Tradition*. Chapel Hill: University of North Carolina Press. [Google Scholar]

ROC United (Restaurant Opportunities Centers United). 2019. *Building the High Road to Racial Equity: Addressing Implicit Bias in the San Francisco Bay Area Restaurant Industry*. https://chapters.rocunited.org/wp-content/uploads/2019/06/TheHighRoad_RacialEquity_Report.pdf. [Google Scholar]

Roman-Alcalá, A. 2020. "Agrarian Anarchism and Authoritarian Populism: Towards a More (State-)Critical 'Critical Agrarian Studies'." *The Journal of Peasant Studies*, May, 1–31. doi:10.1080/03066150.2020.1755840. [Taylor & Francis Online], [Web of Science®], [Google Scholar]

Rosset, P. M., B. Machín Sosa, A. M. Roque Jaime, and D. R. Ávila Lozano. 2011. "The *Campesino-to-Campesino* Agroecology Movement of ANAP in Cuba: Social Process Methodology in the Construction of Sustainable Peasant Agriculture and Food Sovereignty." *Journal of Peasant Studies* 38 (1): 161–191. doi:10.1080/03066150.2010.538584. [Taylor & Francis Online], [Web of Science®], [Google Scholar]

Sachs, C., and A. Patel-Campillo. 2014. "Feminist Food Justice: Crafting a New Vision." *Feminist Studies* 40 (2): 396–410. doi:10.15767/feministstudies.40.2.396. [Crossref], [Web of Science®], [Google Scholar]

Samuel, S. 2020. "The Meat We Eat is a Pandemic Risk, Too." *Vox*, April 22. [Google Scholar]

Saxena, J. 2020. "The Livelihoods of Food-service Workers are Completely Uncertain." *Eater*, March 18. [Google Scholar]

Schanzenbach, D. W., and A. Pitts. 2020. "Estimates of Food Insecurity during the COVID-19 Crisis: Results from the COVID Impact Survey, Week 1 (April 20–26, 2020). Institute for Policy Research Rapid Research." https://www.ipr.northwestern.edu/news/2020/food-insecurity-triples-for-families-during-covid.html. [Google Scholar]

Schanzenbach, D. W., and N. Tomeh. 2020. "Visualizing Food Insecurity." Institute for Policy Research Rapid Research. https://www.ipr.northwestern.edu/documents/reports/ipr-rapid-research-reports-app-visualizes-food-insecurity-14-july-2020.pdf. [Google Scholar]

Schell, C. J., K. Dyson, T. L. Fuentes, S. Des Roches, N. C. Harris, D. S. Miller, C. A. Woelfle-Erskine, and M. R. Lambert. 2020. "The Ecological and Evolutionary Consequences of Systemic Racism in Urban Environments." *Science*, August. doi:10.1126/science.aay4497. [Crossref], [PubMed], [Web of Science®], [Google Scholar]

Schlosser, E. 2001. "The Most Dangerous Job in America." *Mother Jones*, July/August. [Google Scholar]

Schlosser, E. 2020. "America's Slaughterhouses aren't Just Killing Animals." *The Atlantic*, May 12. [Google Scholar]

Schneider, M. 2017. "Wasting the Rural: Meat, Manure, and the Politics of Agro-Industrialization in Contemporary China." *Geoforum* 78 (January): 89–97. doi:10.1016/j.geoforum.2015.12.001. [Crossref], [Google Scholar]

Schneider, M., and P. McMichael. 2010. "Deepening, and Repairing, the Metabolic Rift." *The Journal of Peasant Studies* 37 (3): 461–484. doi:10.1080/03066150.2010.494371. [Taylor & Francis Online], [Web of Science®], [Google Scholar]

Shattuck, A., C. M. Schiavoni, and Z. VanGelder. 2015. Translating the politics of food sovereignty: Digging into contradictions, uncovering new dimensions. *Globalizations* 12 (4): 421-433.

Singh, M., and N. Lakhani. 2020. "George Floyd Killing: Peaceful Protests Sweep America as Calls for Racial Justice Reach New Heights." *The Guardian*, June 7. [Google Scholar]

Smithfield. 2020. "Smithfield Foods Addresses Misinformation amid COVID-19 Crisis." April 25. https://www.nationalhogfarmer.com/business/smithfield-foods-addresses-misinformation-amid-covid-19-crisis. [Google Scholar]

Snipstal, B. 2015. "Repeasantization, Agroecology and the Tactics of Food Sovereignty." *Canadian Food Studies/La Revue canadienne des études sur l'alimentation* 2 (2): 164–173. doi:10.15353/cfs-rcea.v2i2.132. [Crossref], [Google Scholar]

Soul Fire. 2018. "Reparations Map for Black-Indigenous Farmers." *Soul Fire Farm*, February 2. https://www.soulfirefarm.org/get-involved/reparations/. [Google Scholar]

SSJ (Scholars for Social Justice). 2020. "Defund the Police – An SSJ Webinar on Police, Race, and the University." June 20. https://youtu.be/tLqNP3F5G4w. [Google Scholar]

Sternlicht, A. 2020. "Navajo Nation Has Most Coronavirus Infections Per Capita In US, Beating New York, New Jersey." *Forbes*, May 19. [Google Scholar]

Stewart, E. 2020. "The Essential Worker Trap." *Vox*, May 5. [Google Scholar]

Sun, H., Y. Xiao, J. Liu, D. Wang, F. Li, C. Wang, C. Li, et al. 2020. "Prevalent Eurasian Avian-like H1N1 Swine Influenza Virus with 2009 Pandemic Viral Genes Facilitating Human Infection." *Proceedings of the National Academy of Sciences*, June. doi:10.1073/pnas.1921186117. [Crossref], [Google Scholar]

Tarlau, R. 2020. "Activist Farmers in Brazil Feed the Hungry and Aid the Sick as President Downplays Coronavirus Crisis." *The Conversation*, May 5. [Google Scholar]

Taylor, K.-Y. 2020a. "Of Course There Are Protests. The State is Failing Black People." *The New York Times*, May 29. [Google Scholar]

Taylor, K.-Y. 2020b. "America's Moment of Reckoning': Keeanga-Yamahtta Taylor & Cornel West on Uprising Against Racism." *Democracy Now!* July 3. [Google Scholar]

Thompson, S., and D. Berkowitz. 2020. "USDA Allows Poultry Plants to Raise Line Speeds, Exacerbating Risk of COVID-19 Outbreaks and Injury." *National Employment Law Project*, June 17. [Google Scholar]

Tuckman, J., and R. Booth. 2009. "Four-Year-Old Could Hold Key in Search for Source of Swine Flu Outbreak." *The Guardian*, April 27. [Google Scholar]

Tyson, John H. 2020. "Tyson Ad." *Washington Post*, April 26. https://www.washingtonpost.com/context/tyson-ad/86b9290d-115b-4628-ad80-0e679dcd2669/. [Google Scholar]

UCLA (University of California Los Angeles). 2020. "Divestment Now Demands from UCLA Faculty." June 11. https://ucla.app.box.com/s/sdt4rqz92i0a81l5y53er8jkaegtd9t9. [Google Scholar]

UFCW (United Food and Commercial Workers). 2020. "Trump Order to Keep Meatpacking Plants Open Must Include Immediate Action to Strengthen Coronavirus Testing and Safety Measures." *UFCW Press Release*, April 28. [Google Scholar]

US Congress. 2020. "Text – S.3548 – 116th Congress (2019-2020): CARES Act." https://www.congress.gov/116/bills/s3548/BILLS-116s3548is.pdf. [Google Scholar]

USDA (United States Department of Agriculture). 2019. "2017 Census of Agriculture Highlights: Black Producers." https://www.nass.usda.gov/Publications/Highlights/2019/2017Census_Black_Producers.pdf. [Google Scholar]

USDA-ERS (United States Department of Agriculture Economic Research Service). 2020. "Livestock & Meat Domestic Data, 2019–2020." https://www.ers.usda.gov/data-products/livestock-meat-domestic-data/livestock-meat-domestic-data/#All%20meat%20statistics. [Google Scholar]

US Department of Agriculture. 2018. "US Food-away-from-Home Spending Continued to Outpace Food-at-Home Spending in 2018." http://www.ers.usda.gov/data-products/chart-gallery/gallery/chart-detail/?chartId=58364. [Google Scholar]

USDL (US Department of Labor). 2020. "The Employment Situation: April 2020." *New Release*, Bureau of Labor Statistics, May 8. https://www.bls.gov/news.release/archives/empsit_05082020.htm. [Google Scholar]

USFSA (US Food Sovereignty Alliance). 2018. "Food Sovereignty and Energy Democracy in Just Transitions." October 3. http://usfoodsovereigntyalliance.org/food-sovereignty-and-energy-democracy-in-just-transitions/. [Google Scholar]

Uyeda, R. L. 2020. "A New Native Seed Cooperative Aims to Rebuild Indigenous Foodways." *Civil Eats*. November 10. [Google Scholar]

van den Berg, L., M. B. Goris, J. H. Behagel, G. Verschoor, E. Turnhout, M. I. V. Botelho, and I. Silva Lopes. 2019. "Agroecological Peasant Territories: Resistance and Existence in the Struggle for Emancipation in Brazil." *The Journal of Peasant Studies*, 1–22. doi:10.1080/03066150.2019.1683001. [Taylor & Francis Online], [Web of Science®], [Google Scholar]

Vandermeer, J. H. 2011. *The Ecology of Agroecosystems*. Sudbury, MA: Jones and Bartlett Publishers. [Google Scholar]

van der Ploeg, J. D., D. Barjolle, J. Bruil, G. Brunori, L. M. Costa Madureira, J. Dessein, Z. Drąg, et al. 2019. "The Economic Potential of Agroecology: Empirical

Evidence from Europe." *Journal of Rural Studies* 71 (October): 46–61. doi:10.1016/ j.jrurstud.2019.09.003. [Crossref], [Google Scholar]

Vanloqueren, G., and P. V. Baret. 2009. "How Agricultural Research Systems Shape a Technological Regime that Develops Genetic Engineering but Locks out Agroecological Innovations." *Research Policy* 38 (6): 971–983. doi:10.1016/ j.respol.2009.02.008. [Crossref], [Web of Science®], [Google Scholar]

Wallace, R. 2009a. "The Hog Industry Strikes Back." *Farming Pathogens.* https://farmingpathogens.wordpress.com/2009/06/01/the-hog-industry-strikes-back/. [Google Scholar]

Wallace, R. 2009b. "The NAFTA Flu." *Farming Pathogens.* https://farming-pathogens.wordpress.com/2009/04/28/the-nafta-flu/. [Google Scholar]

Wallace, R. 2020. "Midvinter-19: *On the origins of SARS-CoV-2.*" May 5. https://www.patreon.com/posts/midvinter-19-36797182. [Google Scholar]

Wallace, R. G., R. Kock, L. Bergmann, M. Gilbert, L. Hogerwerf, C. Pittiglio, R. Mattioli, and R. Wallace. 2015. "Did Neoliberalizing West African Forests Produce a New Niche for Ebola?" *International Journal of Health Services* 46 (1): 149–165. doi:10.1177/0020731415611644. [Crossref], [PubMed], [Web of Science®], [Google Scholar]

Wallace, R., A. Liebman, L. Fernado Chaves, and R. Wallace. 2020. "COVID-19 and Circuits of Capital." *Monthly Review*, May 1. [Google Scholar]

Waltenburg, M., T. Victoroff, C. Rose, M. Butterfield, R. Jervis, K. Fedak, J. Gabel, et al. 2020. "CDC Update: COVID-19 Among Workers in Meat and Poultry Processing Facilities – United States, April–May 2020." *MMWR. Morbidity and Mortality Weekly Report* 69 (27): 887–892. doi:10.15585/ mmwr.mm6927e2. [Crossref], [PubMed], [Web of Science®], [Google Scholar]

Walzer, C., and A.Kang. 2020. "Abolish Asia's 'Wet Markets,' Where Pandemics Breed." *Wall Street Journal*, January 27. [Google Scholar]

Wang, C., E. Cheng, and E. Huang. 2020. "Coronavirus Live Updates: Chinese Health Officials Say Death Toll Has Risen to 132." *CNBC*, January 29. https://www.cnbc.com/2020/01/28/coronavirus-live-updates-china-hubei.html. [Google Scholar]

Warner, K., K. Daane, C. Getz, S. Maurano, S. Calderon, and K. Powers. 2011. "The Decline of Public Interest Agricultural Science and the Dubious Future of Crop Biological Control in California." *Agriculture and Human Values* 28 (4): 483–496. doi:10.1007/s10460-010-9288-4. [Crossref], [Web of Science®], [Google Scholar]

Weis, A. J. 2013. *The Ecological Hoofprint: The Global Burden of Industrial Livestock*. London: Zed Books. [Crossref], [Google Scholar]

White, M. M. 2018. *Freedom Farmers: Agricultural Resistance and the Black Freedom Movement*. Chapel Hill: The University of North Carolina Press. [Crossref], [Google Scholar]

White House. 2020. "President Donald J. Trump is Taking Action to Ensure the Safety Of Our Nation's Food Supply Chain." April 28. https://www.whitehouse.gov/briefings-statements/president-donald-j-trump-taking-action-ensure-safety-nations-food-supply-chain/. [Google Scholar]

WHO (World Health Organization). 2020. "Novel Coronavirus – China, Disease Outbreak News." World Health Organization. January 12. http://www.who.int/csr/don/12-january-2020-novel-coronavirus-china/en/. [Google Scholar]

Willett, W., J. Rockström, B. Loken, M. Springmann, T. Lang, S. Vermeulen, T. Garnett, et al. 2019. "Food in the Anthropocene: The EAT–Lancet Commission on Healthy Diets from Sustainable Food Systems." *The Lancet* 393 (10170): 447–492. doi:10.1016/S0140-6736(18)31788-4. [Crossref], [PubMed], [Web of Science®], [Google Scholar]

Wittman, H. 2009. "Reworking the Metabolic Rift: La Vía Campesina, Agrarian Citizenship, and Food Sovereignty." *Journal of Peasant Studies* 36 (4): 805–826. doi:10.1080/03066150903353991. [Taylor & Francis Online], [Web of Science®], [Google Scholar]

Wittman, H., A. A. Desmarais, and N. Wiebe, eds. 2010. *Food Sovereignty: Reconnecting Food, Nature and Community*. Oakland, CA: Food First Books.

WMHC (Wuhan Municipal Health Commission). 2019. "Wuhan Municipal Health Commission." http://wjw.wuhan.gov.cn/front/web/showDetail/20191231089. [Google Scholar]

World Food Programme. 2020. "WFP Chief Warns of Hunger Pandemic as COVID-19 Spreads." Statement to UN Security Council, World Food Programme, April 21. https://www.wfp.org/news/wfp-chief-warns-hunger-pandemic-covid-19-spreads-statement-un-security-council. [Google Scholar]

Wu, J., W. Cai, D. Watkins, and J. Glanz. 2020. "How the Virus Got Out." *The New York Times*, March 22. [Google Scholar]

Wu, P., X. Hao, E. Lau, J. Wong, K. Leung, J. Wu, B. Cowling, and G. Leung. 2020. "Real-time Tentative Assessment of the Epidemiological Characteristics of Novel Coronavirus Infections in Wuhan, China." *Eurosurveillance* 25

(3), doi:10.2807/1560-7917.ES.2020.25.3.2000044. [Crossref], [Web of Science®], [Google Scholar]

Yaffe-Bellany, D., and M. Corkery. 2020. "Dumped Milk, Smashed Eggs, Plowed Vegetables: Food Waste of the Pandemic." *The New York Times*, April 11. [Google Scholar]

Yglesias, M. 2020. "8 can't Wait, Explained." *Vox*, June 5. [Google Scholar]

Zhang, Q., and J. Donaldson. 2008. "The Rise of Agrarian Capitalism with Chinese Characteristics: Agricultural Modernization, Agribusiness and Collective Land Rights." *The China Journal* 60: 25–47. doi:10.1086/tcj.60.20647987. [Crossref], [Web of Science®], [Google Scholar]

Zhang, T., Q. Wu, and Z. Zhang. 2020. "Probable Pangolin Origin of SARS-CoV-2 Associated with the COVID-19 Outbreak." *Current Biology* 30 (7): 1346–1351.e2. doi:10.1016/j.cub.2020.03.022. [Crossref], [PubMed], [Web of Science®], [Google Scholar]

Zhou, P., H. Fan, T. Lan, X.-L. Yang, W.-F. Shi, W. Zhang, Y. Zhu, et al. 2018. "Fatal Swine Acute Diarrhoea Syndrome Caused by an HKU2-Related Coronavirus of Bat Origin." *Nature* 556 (7700): 255–258. doi:10.1038/s41586-018-0010-9. [Crossref], [PubMed], [Web of Science®], [Google Scholar]

Acknowledgements

An earlier version of this article appeared in *The Journal of Peasant Studies*. A University of California Presidential Postdoctoral Fellowship partly supported this work. I would like to thank Rob Wallace for sharpening points on pandemic ecologies and three anonymous peer reviewers who did their good work to improve the effort. An especially big thanks to SA Smythe, Nick Mitchell, Charmaine Chua, Hannah Appel, Erin Debenport, Amy Ritterbusch, Joshua Clover, Jennifer Kelly, Jessica Taft, the UC Santa Cruz graduate students, and many other UC workers for sharing their expertises on abolition and welcoming me into organizing spaces. Any errors in the analysis or otherwise are purely my own.

About the author

Maywa Montenegro de Wit is a transdisciplinary researcher working at the intersection of agroecology, political ecology, and science & technology studies on questions broadly related to transformations to equitable food systems. As an assistant professor in the department of Environmental Studies at UC Santa Cruz, she braids a background in molecular biology and science journalism into critical social science approaches to food systems research and education. Current teaching and research interests include gene editing in agriculture, commoning alternatives to IP, abolitionist praxis, and knowledge politics of agroecology and food sovereignty movements globally.

A first-generation US citizen, Dr. Montenegro was raised in rural Appalachia and is the daughter of an Indigenous Quechua father and a Dutch mother. Her PhD work at UC Berkeley explored trends of agrobiodiversity loss through the lens of colonialism, the Green Revolution, and knowledge politics shaping contemporary landscapes of dispossession and repossession. Her postdoc at UC Davis extended this research into CRISPR/Cas gene editing in food systems, specifically how discourses of "democratization" enable contradictory possibilities to unfold in the making, sharing, and governing of new technologies. As a new professor at UC Santa Cruz, she is continuing to research new biotechnologies, pathways connecting agrobiodiversity to human health/nutrition, and agroecological-abolitionist food futures. Dr. Montenegro is an Associate Editor for the *Journal of Agroecology and Sustainable Food Systems*, serves on the board of the *Journal of Agriculture and Human Values*, and co-facilitates the *Agroecology Research-Action Collective* (ARC).

CPSIA information can be obtained
at www.ICGtesting.com
Printed in the USA
LVHW050505301222
736156LV00002B/358

9 781990 263033